The Winning Dad

The Winning Dad

How to Finish First with Your Kids

Stan Toler

and

Jerry Brecheisen

With a Foreword by Dale Jarrett

Indianapolis, Indiana

Copyright 2003 by The Wesleyan Church.

Published by Wesleyan Publishing House
Indianapolis, Indiana 46250

Printed in the United States of America.
ISBN 0-89827-257-2

To my sons, Seth Aaron Toler and Adam James Toler. A father couldn't ask for better sons. You make me proud every day!

STAN TOLER

To my father, Loren Brecheisen, for his sacrificial life, his constant concern, and his dedicated ministry.

To my sons-in-law, Troy Cundiff and Jeff Eckart, for their devotion to my daughters and my grandchildren.

To my friend and neighbor, Gary Patton, whose commitment to his family motivated his life until its untimely end.

To my daughters, Mandi and Arianna, who patiently loved me while I learned how to be a dad.

And to my wife, Carol, for love and loyalty beyond measure.

JERRY BRECHEISEN

Contents

In racing, every little bit helps. From shaving a few seconds off a pit stop to getting just the right tire combination, attention to detail often makes the difference between celebrating in the winner's circle after the race and packing up and heading home.

If you're a dad like me, you want to be the very best. But these days, getting to victory lane is challenging. It's difficult to be a good dad even in the best of times, and today we have few points of reference for the challenges we're facing.

Simply said, most of us have never been in this situation before. Oh, I've heard the expression, "Son, when I was your age, I. . . ." But dads today know deep in their hearts that there's never been a time quite like this. From the fallen towers in New York City to the rising tide of immoral lifestyles, this is truly a new day.

I honestly believe that if I didn't have a spiritual anchor, it would be much more difficult to deal with the many uncertainties we face today. My faith in God has changed my life. As a father, I have a source of strength that never needs refueling!

I learned that faith from my own mom and dad. My parents taught me by example about the thing that matters most—a relationship with the Lord. I have received many accolades throughout my career, but I'm honored most by the opportunity to pass along my parents' spiritual values to my own children.

I am also really thankful for the fellow drivers, owners, and crewmembers who are willing to put their faith—as well as their lives—on the line. We share a bond that is greater than any business relationship or intense competition. We are a family that not only weeps together over common losses but also triumphs together in shared victories. And we're very blessed to have an organization like Motor Racing Outreach that provides us with spiritual support at home and at the track. They encourage us to be our very best, and they know that our greatest victory comes when we lay down our racing helmets and pick up the sword of faith, the Bible, to teach our children and our children's children about the most important finish line in life.

The T-shirt slogan read, *Dads: No Instructions Needed.* It was spotted in the clearance section of a discount store on the Saturday before Father's Day—right next to the *I'm With Stupid* and *I'm Stupid* T-shirt ensemble.

And rightly so!

Any dad who thinks he doesn't need a little help moving through the traffic of these times should probably add all three shirts to his wardrobe.

NASCAR owners, drivers, and crewmembers would be the first to admit that a little fatherly advice doesn't hurt. Indianapolis sportswriter Scott MacGregor describes their lifestyle as a "tug-of-war between professional obligations—practice, qualifying, sponsor meetings, autograph signings—and family time." He adds, "Drivers say the NASCAR schedule can be brutal on family life—thirty-eight weekends away from home, including twenty consecutive to end the season. . . . Of the top drivers in Winston Cup, twenty-nine have children—as do dozens more crewmembers, souvenir vendors, motor-home drivers and other members of the NASCAR traveling show."[1] Brickyard winner and father of two Bobby Labonte adds, "It takes a beating on us."[2]

But many dads have accepted this grueling challenge—and excelled! They're winning dads, who have discovered the winning combination of faith and family. And they're getting more than a little help from their friends at Motor Racing Outreach

(MRO). With chapel services conducted by one of ten full-time chaplains, Bible studies, daycare for children, a traveling workout facility, and a "bleacher ministry" to the multiplied thousands of fans, it makes an eternal impact on the lives of dads who spend their lives running in circles at speeds up to 200 miles per hour.

Founded by well-known drivers and owners, this organization has been a stabilizing force in the fast and frenzied world of auto, motorcycle, and powerboat racing. With thanks to them for their cooperative effort, we offer some practical help to a very special group of competitors—dads.

We know that stock car drivers are not the only ones going full speed down the straightaway. Twenty-first century family life is running at warp speed. Check the door of almost any refrigerator. Next to the works of art in progress from kindergartners and snapshots of junior high athletes in progress, there is probably a calendar with more marks on it than a bowler's scorecard.

In between the karate class on Monday and the soccer game on Saturday, modern dads and moms have a brief opportunity to complete the priceless task of raising their children. In what seems like just minutes a week, they must influence their kids to be stellar citizens on earth and future residents of heaven.

Whew!

This book, by the way, is one *without* all the answers. But it does have a few. And those come from the owner's manual for human life, the Bible, and from some faithful dads who have learned how to balance a race car in one hand and a family in the other. There are *Dad Tips* by members of NASCAR racing teams, quotable quotes from standout drivers, owners, and crewmembers, and chapter-by-chapter helps for present and future fathers.

The authors, too, have been around the track a few times. Not in a three-thousand-pound stock car—they've only seen that kind of action from the stands. But they've been gathering dad points on the busy (and often hazardous) streets of life. With children and grandchildren of their own, they know how important it is to pick up some tips that will help avoid a crash.

The Winning Dad is a book for you—whether you're on this side of the altar or the other side of the picket fence. It's dedicated to providing the insight you'll need to respond with grace when Sissy wipes out the first row of canned corn at the grocery store or when Junior comes home with a new girlfriend who might have the starring role in a science fiction movie. We hope these pages will be as practical as lug nuts on a racing rim and as refreshing as bottled water in Thunder Alley.

So go ahead. Flip the starter switch. Then listen for Heaven's Spotter on the radio of your heart and hit the throttle. You can finish first with your family!

STAN TOLER AND JERRY BRECHEISEN

 **Special Thanks**

To friend and publisher Don Cady and the staff of Wesleyan Publishing House.

To Billy Mauldin, Ron Pegram, and Cheryl Shore of Motor Racing Outreach for their kind assistance with this project.

To Kelley Jarrett, Beth Hart, Randy MacDonald, Wayne Richards, and Jim Weinmann for editorial and technical assistance.

To Deloris Leonard and Pat Diamond for editorial assistance.

To Lawrence Wilson for his great editorial skills and brotherly friendship.

Coy Gibbs Plans to Follow Dad's Tradition

NASCAR driver Coy Gibbs and his wife, Heather, are parents of a newborn son, Ty. Pointing to a family tradition established by his father, Joe Gibbs, Coy plans to send regular letters of encouragement, correction, and instruction from the Bible to his son in the years ahead. Coy knows the value of giving his son support in achieving personal goals, yet he plans to give Ty "room to choose his own path." He adds, "I don't want to push him." Coy Gibbs credits his spiritual upbringing in church and in Christian schools for developing his own walk with the Lord. He passes that heritage along to other young people by regularly sharing his faith with teens in high school assemblies.

Winning Dad Tip

Give your child freedom to make personal decisions.

■■■■■■■■■■■■■■■■ *Racer's Edge*

*Winning dads
have bold faith in
troubled times.*

Drivers Wanted
The Challenge of Being a Dad

 *The most important thing a parent can do is to
ensure that their children are brought up in
church and that they hear the Word of God,
especially when they're young.*

—Robert Pressley, NASCAR Driver

He's not a bad father, he's just a stupid man doing the best job
he can."

The commercial for yet another father-bashing sitcom played
on network television. The hapless "father" stood by with an
armful of children and a dopey expression while his "wife"
ridiculed him in front of millions. I wonder what he was thinking?
The actor, that is. I wonder what his impression of fatherhood was
after playing the role that had been scripted for him?

Family roles are changing. It really is a new day for dads. The parenting racetrack is different now. The familiar oval is gone—the dependable, traditional role of a father. It's a road course now. There are bends and turns that dads of yesterday could never have imagined.

Do you remember Ozzie and Harriet? In their era, the fifties, it would have been criminal to publicly rebel against Dad. The new Ozzie changed all that. Twenty-first-century Ozzie (Osbourne, that is) suffers the criticisms and curses of his family on network television, and the ratings have climbed higher than the volume on their profanity-filled set.

Things Have Changed

Father bashing has become something like an Olympic event these days. A *USA Today* article explains why: "With political correctness putting an ever increasing portion of the population off limits for humorous situations, advertisers are increasingly casting straight males as folks who can't cook, drive, or watch the kids without making a mess of it."[1] Did you get it? Dads are getting bashed simply because there's no one left to take the hit!

In spite of the sitcom scorn, there are scores of dads who are dedicated to doing the job—and doing it right, for the most part. They're nine-to-five examples of hard work, loyalty, and love, living in a post–nine-eleven age. They are reaching deep inside for the courage, conviction, and character to be the best examples they can be to their families. And they're doing it in a road-course age, successfully maneuvering the twists and turns of a brand new day.

What's changed? Here's a survey of today's parenting landscape.

*A dad is a man who carries photographs
where his money used to be!*

—James S. Hewitt

Fragmented Families

The traditional home is about as rare today as the traditional fireplace. Hours of chopping wood have been replaced by an instant flipping of the starter switch on a gas log. The new work ethic promises—and delivers—maximum benefit for minimum effort. For example, today's fast-food employee earns more per hour by leveraging french fries than yesterday's scientists did for making lifesaving discoveries.

The family is different as well. Scenes like Robert Young and Jane Wyatt sitting around the table sharing dinner with Buddy, Sissy, and Kathy on *Father Knows Best* are about as rare today as a live bug on the windshield of a stock car. Twenty-first century families seem to be playing Bingo by racing to fill in the squares on the kitchen calendar.

Television-style families like the Nelsons and Andersons are history. The new family has arrived. The last government census revealed that single-mother families grew from 12 percent of all families in 1970 to 26 percent in 2000. And single-father families increased from 1 percent of the total in 1970 to 5 percent in 2000.

Some of those new family units are struggling—especially in today's uncertain financial climate. According to Crown Financial Ministries, "Most single mothers earn a little above poverty level income. And 20 percent of single fathers live at the poverty level. In 1996, when welfare reform was enacted, 87 percent of the recipients of benefits lived in single parent households."[2] So the comic spin on the Disney lyric, *I owe, I owe, so off to work I go,* is nearly a national anthem.

The result: latchkey kids are raising themselves, slurping Big Gulps on the way home from school and "nuking" macaroni and cheese between cell phone calls. And the home-alone lifestyle has taken a toll. Statistics on alcoholism and unwanted pregnancy now include grade-schoolers!

Degrading Entertainment

A TB test may indicate the presence of an infectious disease in the body. A *TV* test might reveal an infectious disorder in society. The TV culture has influenced the new family in an unprecedented way. Families spend from four to six hours a day watching sitcom or "reality" shows, or playing electronic kill-'em games. As a result, an entire generation has failed to learn how to speak. Have you ever listened to a TV-generation superstar being interviewed by a reporter?

The messages delivered by the entertainment media are as contagious as they are deadly. Sexy, short-attention-span entertainment is in. Advocates for alternative lifestyles don't need to buy airtime. They simply weave their godless philosophies into programs that target young minds. Gross has become acceptable and immorality the norm.

Computer "Communication"

Remember the Commodore 64? No, it wasn't a singing group. This product marked the dawn of new day for thinking, writing, and keeping track of details. It ushered in the age of personal computing. And sometime after that, the computer mouse cannibalized the No. 2 lead pencil.

Life has never been the same. Banks now have a hole in the wall where people can retrieve money twenty-four hours a day, and personal identities have been reduced to a string of zeroes and ones. People can "talk" to each other without talking to each other. Porn shops have For Sale signs on their front doors—they've moved to the Internet, where anyone with a credit card can buy their filthy wares on a trial basis.

It's estimated that we send up to a trillion E-mail messages each year. There are over two billion Internet pages now available, and more are added each day. Our society has a severe case of Inflammatory Informationitis.

The result is a generation of socially deficient children. Today's kids are computer savvy but relationship challenged. They can surf the Internet with their eyes closed, but many have the personality of a doorstop. And why not? You don't have to talk to a computer monitor! The lack of communication in this Communication Age is a problem. We can load the music that used to fill a ceiling-high stack of vinyl albums into a digital device the size of a wristwatch—but we've forgotten how to whistle.

A father to the fatherless, a defender of widows, is God in his holy dwelling.

—Psalm 68:5

Cultural Diversity

The inscription on Lady Liberty's concrete pedestal says as much about the times as it does about citizenship. "Give me your tired" could be a commentary on today's societal soup. The culture is wearily changing. Our population is becoming both grayer and more colorful—older and less Anglo-Saxon. As a result, you may observe Baby Boomers struggling to understand a hip-hop lyric or see a frustrated Burger King employee trying to explain "super size" to an English-challenged immigrant.

Learning new languages.

Understanding new cultures.

Getting used to new clothing styles.

These days it's hard to tell whether the average man on the street is displaying a new fashion fad or whether he happened to be walking by a Goodwill store when it exploded.

Families have been mixed into this new cultural casserole. The classroom isn't the same. The workplace is different. The playground has a new look. The mall has a whole new atmosphere. And the home is feeling the effects of it all.

Terrorism

Face it, all the debris from the World Trade Center has not yet been removed. Some of the dust is still in the air. To say that our lives will never be the same is an understatement. Financially, politically, socially, emotionally, and spiritually, our familiar institutions have become triage centers for the walking wounded. We've been nine-elevened.

We've become a society that looks over its shoulder. Suspicion has replaced consideration. We train our children to doubt first and delight later. We ask them to grow up in a world that's waiting for the other shoe to drop, then we wonder why they see monsters under the bed at night.

Political Correctness

The new family lives in an awkward time. Thanks to Jell-O–spined politicos, our kids don't even know where to pledge their allegiance. God has been given a note by the teacher and sent to study hall. And trying to say the correct thing about anyone or anything has become as awkward as clipping a centipede's toenails with chopsticks. Families wonder whose rights are right—and what rights are left! It's getting so that paying a compliment could draw a fine. Our children are confused. Political correctness has become Houdini's straight jacket. We've been turned upside down, and we're searching for the way out!

It is easier to build boys than to mend men.

—Albert Wells, Jr.

Dads Are Still Winning

Fortunately, the culture cloud has a silver lining. In spite of all the changes, dads are reaching within themselves and pulling out their very best. The times may be different, but the resolve in their hearts is greater than ever. Like determined stock car racers, they're pulling onto pit road and making alignment adjustments, then making bold moves back onto the track.

Like the biblical David's inner circle of bravest soldiers, David's Mighty Men, today's dads are ready for the challenge—

- Ready to mold young minds and warm young hearts.
- Ready to trust the power and promises of God.
- Ready to give their lives to a living Christ, following Him

as if nothing else matters and discovering that nothing else really does.

How are they doing it? What's their race day strategy? Here are some traits of a winning dad.

Bold Faith

Tim Shutt, car chief for the #18 MBNA Busch Series car said, "At about twenty years old, a friend of mine asked me to go to a Bible study. I agreed and went. At that point I knew what was missing: the Lord Jesus Christ. I gave everything to Him, and it has made the biggest difference in my life to this day. I no longer search; my life is complete with Christ."[1] Tim had grown up in a Christian home, but until he made a personal commitment to Jesus Christ, he was still searching for something to trust. Secondhand faith didn't work.

Tim discovered that he had to *personally* accept Christ's invitation to follow Him. Tim answered the challenge with his own life, just like those who followed Jesus in Bible times. "As Jesus was walking beside the Sea of Galilee, he saw two brothers, Simon called Peter and his brother Andrew. They were casting a net into the lake, for they were fishermen. 'Come, follow me,' Jesus said, 'and I will make you fishers of men.' At once they left their nets and followed him" (Matthew 4:18–20).

Robert Pressley said it's important for dads to "ensure that their children . . . hear the word of God, especially when they're young." He didn't drag his kids to church. He took them. It was the practice of his faith that proved his own relationship with Christ.

You may have heard people say that when they were young, they had a "drug problem"—they were *drug* to school, *drug* to the dentist, and *drug* to church. Faith is better discovered than "drugged." Being force fed the faith is like eating cactus. You may swallow it, but it won't feel good!

Clear Example

A sportswriter said of NBA superstar David Robinson: "In a profession known for its excess, the multimillion dollar man is cautious about where he lends his name and spends his fame. Jesus and his family come first, he says, then basketball. He is more concerned that his three boys learn godly character than whether they can match his top-ten ranking in the NBA for points, rebounds, and blocked shots per game. He is more concerned that his fans see him live out his faith than he is interested in talking about the time in 1994 that he scored seventy-one points against the Los Angeles Clippers."[2]

I don't remember my dad reading any owners' manuals. I never saw him sitting in a lounge chair studying how to change the dome light of his station wagon or fix the on/off switch on the dishwasher. As a matter of fact, Dad couldn't have finished either project without the help of the entire staff of a Sears service center!

What I do remember is this: often when I awakened early in the morning, I entered the living room to find Dad sitting in his chair by the bay window, reading his Bible and his favorite devotional book.

That clear example made a lasting impression. My Dad influenced me by openly practicing his faith. First-person faith makes a second-tier impression. A past-forgiven, future-assured relationship with God can't be kept undercover. Personal faith shouldn't be kept in the garage like a semi-restored Volkswagen bus. It needs to be on the road, running hard like a diesel pickup. And that kind of faith always casts a positive shadow. Our kids

will need that kind of faith—

- When buildings blow up.
- When floods rage.
- When Dow Jones dives.
- When world tempers rise.

When life is at its worst, they'll need faith at its best. Dads, you can show it to them! With God's help, you can set a spiritual example that's as refreshing as a cold glass of milk and a plate of warm chocolate chip cookies.

Raw Courage

About an hour's drive from the famed motor speedway in Indianapolis, there is a forty–acre campground. It's a work in progress. There's a recreation building. A kitchen. Some cabins. A basketball court (almost a requirement in Indiana). Restrooms and showers. A few campsites. Soon there'll be a swimming pool and a stocked lake.

It's a camp dedicated to serving underprivileged children. The owners, a husband-and-wife team, have a clear purpose. "Our goal is to put a smile on a kid's face," they'll tell you.

In the office hangs a picture of a race car driver. It's proudly encased behind glass, standing out from several racing trophies. It's a photo of NASCAR great Kenny Irwin Jr., who died in a racing accident at the age of thirty. Kenny's mom and dad are building the camp in his memory.

Also featured prominently in the camp office is Kenny's motto: "Dare to Dream." On the day Kenny died, one dream seemed to die with him. But another rose from the wreckage. He had touched thousands of people through his life. In his memory, the camp will touch thousands more. Kenny Irwin Sr. said that his son "knew it was a privilege to be in this sport and he felt an urgency to give back."

Not that it's easy for his parents. They still grieve the loss. "No one can tell you the pain you go through," says Kenny's dad. "There are times when you are so busy with life, you don't notice. . . . but then there's other times when the littlest thing will bring everything back." Completing the campground has been a challenge for the Irwins, but one they've gladly accepted for Kenny's sake. "We've dared ourselves," they said.[3]

Others have dared as well. You've seen examples of their raw courage in everyday acts of heroism.

A friend dies; a good man, a good husband and father. You watch as another dad—a relative or friend—picks up the pieces of a broken family by mowing the grass, changing the oil, or taking a fatherless boy to a football game.

Another family faces financial hardship. There's a bankruptcy, in spite of careful planning. A bewildered dad stands on the rubble of a thousand dreams, holding a layoff notice in his hands and asking "Why?" Then that father goes into recovery mode—making sacrifices, cutting back, working extra hours at a part-time job. No amount of corporate downsizing can shrink Dad's heart. He'll fight like a tiger to provide for his family.

A marriage fails. Vows are left at the altar, and estranged partners go in search of missing persons. The family room gives way to the divorce court, and it may be dad who is left to do the tucking in, the bedtime praying, the sandwich making—and the horrible explaining. He rises to the challenge.

The high banks on some racetracks are now lined with "soft walls"—Styrofoam padding that's supposed to absorb some of the shock in a crash. But even soft walls can't always prevent an injury or the painful recovery that follows. Many dads have experienced a crash—and the pain that comes with it. They've "traded paint" with a few walls themselves.

But dads by the score have discovered a faith that dares to dream in spite of tragedy, a faith that builds a milestone over a mess. Winning dads survive third-degree calamities. They know that God has promised His peace, His presence, and His power for emergency times. They realize that times of testing can result in personal and spiritual growth.

You're on the Right Track

Granted, being a dad can be hazardous to your health. As Ogden Nash said, "A family is a unit composed not only of children, but of men, women, an occasional animal, and the common cold." Sometimes, the cold is the lesser of the worries.

Dad, when you first held that newborn in your arms, you didn't think about the sleeplessness that he or she would cause later on. You didn't realize that you'd someday lie awake listening for the sound of the family car in the driveway and wondering which fender would bear the marks of an automotive encounter.

You didn't visualize the fall-from-the-bicycle cut that would take you to the emergency room where the surgeon would stitch your bundle of joy while you held the screaming patient to your chest, praying that you wouldn't pass out in front of the nurse.

Little did you realize then that you'd experience your own heart pains as that child was rejected by another—especially by a pimply-faced teen with an adenoid problem.

But neither did you realize all of the resources God had already made available for you. You didn't know about the sufficiency of His grace. You couldn't have fathomed the depths of love or the heights of mercy that He would add to your parenting skills.

Now you know that your heavenly Father is committed to assisting with your earthly assignment. He'll be with you from the pace lap through the finish line—and every yellow flag in between.

You can rise to this challenge!

- Teach your child how to obey before you teach him how to ride a bike.
- Give your child words of encouragement rather than unjust criticisms.
- Focus your child's attention on eternal truth rather than fleeting fables.
- Love unconditionally, praise unreservedly, and give unexpectedly.

Before you know it, the hospital gown that was open at the back will be replaced with a rented tuxedo that's too wide in the shoulders, too small in the waist, and—you can count on it—missing one cuff link. You're going to make it, Dad! Heaven's on your side and your teammates are running with you. You *can* finish first as a dad!

Time Is a Balancing Act for David Green

Career Highlights

- 1994 Busch Series Champion
- 19 Career pole positions
- National Champion, World Karting Association (Senior Class)
- Winston Cup and Busch Series driver

David Green says being a NASCAR driver makes it "triple tough" to balance work and family time. "There are always lots of odds and ends that need to be taken care of," Green says of life at the track. When not driving in the Winston Cup or Busch Series, Green is a spotter for Dale Jarrett's #88 car. "But my main job is being a dad," David says. During one interval between testing cars, he began to realize what a short period of time he would have with his family and faced a tough personal decision about what mattered most. "I asked myself, 'What can I do better?'" David says. The answer? He determined to set aside quality time for his family. "Family life is a balancing act," the former Busch champion says. He's set the balance in favor of wife, Diane, and his children, Kaylie and Austin.

Winning Dad Tip

Manage your time so that you can be there for your family.

You Have a Sponsor
God's Plan for Dads

God can take your need and bless you, as well as others around you, if you put Him first.

—Darrell Waltrip, Three-Time Winston Cup Champion

Before a NASCAR driver can reach the starting grid, he needs to acquire several things—including a ride. Obviously, a race car driver needs something to race. And before that racing vehicle ever gets to the garage, it'll need a sponsor. You've seen those stock cars and trucks, speckled with more logos than pepper on a Virginia ham. And you've seen the driver uniforms as well. Sponsor brand names are stitched over almost every square inch of fabric, making you wonder how the poor guy can find the zipper in a hurry!

Those animated billboards indicate that someone has supplied the resources to fund the ride. The team has a sponsor.

Depending on the amount invested, the sponsor's logo may be more or less prominently displayed. On his web site, Craftsman Truck Series driver Randy MacDonald has an illustrated guide for sponsors. A diagram shows the prime locations reserved for "title sponsors": the top of the truck, the hood, truck bed, upper tailgate, and upper side panels. "Associate sponsors" display smaller logos in less prominent spaces on the vehicle.

The display possibilities don't end with the track vehicle. MacDonald's sponsors can place logos on the eighteen-wheel transporter, garage board, pit wall signs, and even the pit box.

When you add team uniforms, ball caps, T-shirts, jackets, cups and mugs, the opportunities for sponsor recognition are nearly endless.

Benefits of God's Sponsorship

Dad, you may say, "I wish I had a sponsor!" First of all, it's doubtful that your boss would want you to arrive for work with all those logo patches on your clothes—even if the dress code is business casual!

Second, you *do* have a sponsor. Your heavenly Father has already committed His resources to support your laps around life's track. Hopefully, you are displaying His sponsorship prominently—with your smile, in your work, and by your words and deeds. You're not alone in the race to raise godly children. God has promised all the help you need to succeed.

Here are some of the resources God has provided for dads. Think of them as perks from the perfect Sponsor.

His Son

A Winston Cup car owner once estimated that it costs more

than $15 million to sponsor a team for one season. That's a big investment! But it's nothing compared to God's resources. For one thing, He gave you His son.

One of the most memorable verses in the Bible reminds us, "For God so loved the world that he gave his one and only Son, that whoever believes in him shall not perish but have eternal life" (John 3:16). You might call that the most costly sponsorship ever! God gave His precious son to become your title sponsor.

And that was no small investment. About God's Son, Jesus, the Bible says this:

> He is the image of the invisible God, the firstborn over all creation. For by him all things were created: things in heaven and on earth, visible and invisible, whether thrones or powers or rulers or authorities; all things were created by him and for him. He is before all things, and in him all things hold together (Colossians 1:15–17).

All the wealth of heaven was summed up in one person: Jesus. And God gave His life to ensure your victory. That sponsorship is important for several reasons.

An Example of Love. First, it shows that God loves us. Some people see God as a cartoon caricature—a rickety old man wearing a flowing white robe and a long scraggily beard, carrying a sign that reads, "Repent, the end is near." Considering recent world events, the message on the cartoonist's sign may be worth more than a passing thought! But that image of God as a prophet of doom is grossly in error.

Contrary to popular opinion, God is more concerned with getting you to heaven than sending you to hell. He wants to be your mentor, not your tormentor. He's sponsored you to win!

Here's good news: God is on your side! Everyone in your carpool may plot against you, but God is for you. He wants you to succeed as a dad. He wants to stand beside you in Victory Lane with His loving arm around you and whisper in your ear, "I told you we'd win!"

An Example of Fatherhood. Another reason God's sponsorship is important is that it shows us how to be a father. His relationship with His Son, Jesus Christ, is Fatherhood 101 for today's dads.

We get a glimpse of good parenting at Jesus' baptism, where His Father lavished approval on Him. The Bible says: "As soon as Jesus was baptized, he went up out of the water. At that moment heaven was opened, and he saw the Spirit of God descending like a dove and lighting on him. And a voice from heaven said, 'This is my Son, whom I love; with him I am well pleased'" (Matthew 3:16–17). That's a loving Dad!

We get another insight into parenting from Jesus' perfect prayer, the Lord's Prayer. Jesus said, "This, then, is how you should pray: 'Our Father in heaven, hallowed be your name'" (Matthew 6:9). Jesus understood that His father loved Him. Obviously, God did a great job of communicating His affection to His child.

"Then how come the heavenly Father let His Son die?" you may ask.

Because He also loves *you*. There was no way to fulfill the requirement of God's perfect and eternal law except to give a perfect and eternal sacrifice for your sin. God, the brokenhearted Father, paid the ultimate price. And that wonderful act shows us something else about being a good dad—our commitment to our family must be without limits.

An Example of Eternal Values. Additionally, God's sponsorship shows us how important it is to put stock in the eternal. That's something we already know, but we need periodic reminders. Today's investments are tomorrow's payoffs. We must major on the things that last forever.

- Loving firmness today pays off in an obedient behavior tomorrow.

- Affirmation of a child today pays off in a confident adult tomorrow.

- Building character today pays off in growing influence tomorrow.

- Love and loyalty today pay off in respect and trust tomorrow.

Remember that racing sponsors have no intention of underwriting last place finishes. They invest in *winners* not *whiners!* God wants you to win, so He has committed all of His resources to helping you succeed as a dad.

His Word

You have another resource for being a dad. You have God's Word, the Bible. Your Title Sponsor has given you a written guarantee of His support. Nearly forty biblical authors came to the same conclusion over a span of 1600 years—God loves you!

No wonder their God-breathed (inspired) work is the best-selling book of all time! And no wonder Darrell Waltrip saw the need for Bible study as one reason to support the creation of Motor Racing Outreach. He said, "A need that Lake Speed, Bobby Hillin and myself had was to be able to study the Bible and have fellowship with one another. . . . We watched God take that need and expand it into what [Motor Racing Outreach] is today."[1]

God's Word is one of your greatest resources for holy living.

These are days when making a living seems to take most of our attention. But holy living will always be more important. As Jesus said, "Let your light shine before men, that they may see your good deeds and praise your Father in heaven" (Matthew 5:16).

You're thinking, "Let my light shine? Where's that Energizer bunny when I need it!"

Living a godly life in a world of Internet pornography and corporate thievery seems more difficult than whistling Dixie with a mouth full of Chicken McNuggets. But you *can* live a life that's a cut above ordinary. How? By relying on the advice that God gives in Scripture.

King David said, "How can a young man keep his way pure? By living according to your word. I seek you with all my heart; do not let me stray from your commands. I have hidden your word in my heart that I might not sin against you" (Psalm 119:9–11).

David's question-and-answer combination shows the secret for living a pure life. Dads who do that are those who admit they need help and find it in the Bible. Guiding families through the caution flags of these times takes wisdom you can't find in *TV Guide*. Look to the Book. God's Word will help you.

The Family

The family is another resource God has given fathers. In an age when the definition of family is up for grabs, it's important to remember where it all started.

Eden.

Adam and Eve were God's first family. When He made that original couple and put them in a home that was free from ozone erosion and orthodontist bills, He created something beautiful called a family. Darrell Waltrip recognized the beauty of God's creation when he said, "God showed me just how blessed I was in having such a strong Christian wife, and how children are a true blessing as well."[2]

Touchdown!

God gave us families to bless us not burden us. He knew that we'd need each other to make life bearable, so He provided companionship. Here's how it happened:

The Lord God took the man [Adam] and put him in the Garden of Eden to work it and take care of it. And the Lord God commanded the man, 'You are free to eat from any tree in the garden; but you must not eat from the tree of the knowledge of good and evil, for when you eat of it you will surely die.'

The Lord God said, 'It is not good for the man to be alone. I will make a helper suitable for him.'

Now the Lord God had formed out of the ground all the beasts of the field and all the birds of the air. He brought them to the man to see what he would name them; and whatever the man called each living creature, that was its name. So the man gave names to all the livestock, the birds of the air and all the beasts of the field.

But for Adam no suitable helper was found. So the Lord God caused the man to fall into a deep sleep; and while he was sleeping, he took one of the man's ribs and closed up the place with flesh. Then the Lord God made a woman from the rib he had taken out of the man, and he brought her to the man.

The man said, "This is now bone of my bones and flesh of my flesh; she shall be called 'woman,' for she was taken out of man." For this reason a man will leave his father and mother and be united to his wife, and they will become one flesh" (Genesis 2:15–24).

For Adam, the zoo full of animals that populated the Garden of Eden was not enough company. He needed another person, and God provided her. He still does: father, mother, sister, brother, wife, children—that live-in support system you have was God's idea. He placed us together for a reason. The very people we are responsible *for* are those we are blessed *with!* He knows that we need a hand to hold, so He gave us two—or four, or six, or more!

The family shows us something about God, too. It's as if God has said, "Just as you love and depend on your wife and just as your children depend on you—that's how I want you to relate to me."

The family is part of God's sponsorship package.

One of the best ways to correct your children is to correct the example you are setting for them.

—Talmadge Johnson

The Church

There's one more advantage to God's sponsorship of your family—it's an extended family called the church.

What comes to mind when the word *church* is mentioned? A building with a steeple? A priest or pastor? A Sunday school picnic? A long-winded preacher or a short-fused vacation Bible school teacher?

None of those are the church.

The church is not a collection of bad memories but a vibrant body of believers—people just like you who have placed their trust in Christ. The Bible verse Ephesians 5:23 tells us something about the church: "Christ is the head of the church, his body, of which he is the Savior." Followers of Jesus Christ—those who have trusted Him for forgiveness of the past and hope for the future—are His church.

And what a bunch they are!

- They love each other in spite of their faults.
- They pray for each other in spite of their differences.
- They support each other in spite of their own misfortunes.
- They give to each other in spite of their own needs.

Dad, if you're out on a limb by yourself and think you hear the rev of a McCullough chain saw, remember that you're not alone. God has given you a churchful of teammates.

Maybe you've met some sorry Christians (and they're out there), smiley-faced church members who have their noses so high in the air they might drown in a rainstorm. And you've probably met a hypocrite or two along the way—those who preach one thing and practice another. The church has its share, just like any other human institution. Did you get that? *Human* institution.

But not all the peaches in a bushel have a bad spot, so you don't pick out the blemished ones when you're making cobbler. You focus on the beautiful! And God has a whole company of beautiful people, people who love Him with all their heart and serve Him with all their might. And they are there for you!

- They'll pray for your children.
- They'll counsel you when you have questions.
- They'll give to you when you are in financial need.

Some of them would even die for you. They're Christians, which means Christ-ones. They'll do all of those things because they're copying Jesus Christ.

You may say, "I haven't found any yet." Maybe you're looking in the wrong places—or maybe you're not looking at all. Start with a church that honors Christ and teaches the Bible. Look for those folk who believe that Jesus died on the Cross to pay the price for their past and give them a one-way ticket to the future. Ask around for a good church. Find someone with an honest-to-goodness faith and ask him or her for a referral. You need a support group for raising perfect kids in an imperfect world. You've got it in the church.

Trusting Your Sponsor

It would be foolish to put a race car in competition without a shakedown run. If you were a driver, you wouldn't want to be on the track going over one hundred miles an hour beside, inside, or in front of *anything* that hadn't been through a rigorous inspection. Road testing proves roadworthiness.

That means that the difficult days in which we're living can work to your advantage.

How's that again?

Before you consider sending the authors to the infield infirmary, consider these words: "Blessed is the man who perseveres under trial, because when he has stood the test, he will receive the crown of life that God has promised to those who love him" (James 1:12).

No guts, no glory? No pain, no gain? You're right!

In these extreme times, God provides extraordinary help. When we're "loose" on the track, God's Holy Spirit is in the spotter's chair, giving advice to our spirit. The very dangers we face are part of the deliverance. For example, the faith we gain while praying for a sick child or waiting for news about a layoff is the same faith that will take us through the victory lap.

There are some things you'll need to do too, however.

NFL coach Tony Dungy is not only quick to share his faith, he's also eager to share valuable "dad" tips that he learned from his own father. He says there's a pattern of behavior you'll find in the best dads:

- "They spend time with their children,
- "They are compassionate toward their children,
- "They love and respect their children's mother, and
- "They turn to their faith for strength."[3]

Bob Benson wrote, "The family is just about the place that I want to succeed the most. In fact, I feel that if I fail here, my life will be a failure in spite of everything else that I accomplish, and if I can succeed here, it will somehow atone for all the other failures of my whole life. My most often and fervent prayer is that I will be a successful father."[4]

Dad, there's a lot riding on this race. Your kids need you to finish first. So don't try to run without a sponsor. There's too much at stake. Trust God with your faith, your life, and your family.

He will never leave you without a ride!

Jeff Chandler Says Make Sure Your Kids are Your Friends

Career Highlights

- Mechanic on the #20 Tony Stewart car, Joe Gibbs Racing

Jeff Chandler and his wife, Tammy, are the parents of two children, thirteen-year-old daughter Kristen and ten-year old son Tyler. What dad tip would Jeff give? "Make sure your kids are your friends." Chandler points out that there will be times when parental discipline based on Scriptural principles must be applied. But the responsibilities of parenting also include family bonding times. "Spend time with your kids," Jeff advises. The Chandlers do just that, playing board games, going bowling, and watching movies together as well as having family devotional times when Jeff and Tammy pray with their children.

Winning Dad Tip

Establish some "family time" routines.

*Winning dads take
responsibility for
their families.*

Owner, Driver, Crew Chief
The Roles of a Father

*In racing we have a crew chief and a spotter or two who can talk
to us, so we're not alone in that car. But when you know Christ
and you're in that car, He's in there with you.*

—Jason Keller, NASCAR Driver

You've seen them racing the clock. First, the driver pulls off the
track and aims for the numbered stop sign thrust across his pit
box. Then the seven-member pit crew goes "over the wall" and
begins to work fifteen-second miracles—tire-changing, fuel-adding,
window-washing, alignment-adjusting, duct-tape-applying miracles.

From the moment the race car slams to a halt the pit looks like
a jitterbug support group. Each crewmember has a well-rehearsed
task. Feverishly, the jack man, tire carriers, tire changers, gas-can

man, and catch-can man complete their assigned duties as a NASCAR official circles the pit like a playground monitor, making sure that every "t" is crossed and every "i" is dotted. Meanwhile, the crew chief choreographs the dance through his headset mike, giving orders and listening for signs of trouble.

This dedicated team of technicians is driven by a common goal: get the driver *back on the track.*

Sounds a lot like being a dad, doesn't it?

There's one difference. A father's job is more complicated because he has to fill all those roles at the same time, getting kids race ready to face the world in just over fifteen years!

Dad Wears Many Hats

Miami Herald columnist Leonard Pitts wrote pessimistically that "fatherhood sometimes seems as obsolete as vinyl records. And we don't seem to miss it. To the contrary, it has become fashionable for women to create children expressly without fathers. Has it become routine for those children to say they don't need their fathers, because mother fills both roles?" He adds, "Once upon a time, Father was the indecipherable presence at the head of the table. Then we took away his chair."[1]

But Christian men's organizations like Promise Keepers fill stadiums with men who loudly demand, "Give us back our chair!" The new Christian man, child of the heavenly Father, refuses to relinquish his role as husband, son, brother, and father. And his corner of the world will be a better place because of that stubborn resistance.

That's a far cry from the attitude of one old-timer who was interviewed on his fiftieth wedding anniversary. "Just how did you stay married all these years?" the reporter queried.

The fellow replied, "Well, my wife and I came to an important agreement."

"What's that?"

"It has two parts," the elderly husband continued. "Part one: I agreed that I wouldn't try to run her life."

"And, part two?" the reporter questioned.

"Part two is: I wouldn't try to run mine."

Winning dads don't give up the wheel that easily—especially when it comes to influencing their children. They gladly assume their roles as owner, driver, and crew chief.

How's that?

Dad the Owner

Dad is the owner in the sense that the overall responsibility for the family is his. Just as a racing car, powerboat, or motorcycle owner is responsible to manage the team's total performance—from finances to staffing to race results—dads are responsible for the overall management of their households.

It's a little like the time a child was asked to come to the teacher's desk in English class to discuss her essay on the perfect father. The teacher was very somber: "Sarah, I'm a little surprised at this essay. You're one of my brightest students. But this paper is filled with mistakes. The punctuation is terrible. The spelling is awful. The sentences are weak. What do you think I ought to do about it?"

The young student quickly responded. "I think you ought to give my dad a call. He's the one who wrote it!"

Dads may not be responsible for writing essays about themselves, but they are responsible for many things.

Biblically, dad is the point man for carrying out the will of God by directing his family. The Bible says that a dad must "manage his children and his household well" (1 Timothy 3:12).

Just as racing performance improves with practice, leadership skills are improved by leading. Ken Canfield, founder and president of the National Center for Fathering, writes, "When we work to improve our skills (that is, becoming empathetic toward our children, inspiring them to excellence, exercising control of our behavior, and being open to discuss our own growth as fathers), we are in the process of becoming world-class leaders."[2]

Dads can't possibly manage others until they first learn to manage themselves. A father who follows God's footsteps is more likely to have a family that follows his. Such a dad applies biblical leadership principles to family living—

- He seeks God's direction through prayer and Bible study.
- He expects his children to respect his authority and follow his godly example.
- He affirms the individual abilities of everyone in his family.
- He expresses affection and appreciation.
- He rewards effort with verbal praise.
- He expresses love and devotion to his spouse.

Dad the Driver

Dad is the driver in the sense that he carries out the team's strategy. He is out there on the "track," representing his family. Whether he is on the job or at the gym, he models the values that he teaches at home. What he preaches in private, he practices in public—and not the other way around!

Fads come and go. Each new political campaign is marked by another bumper-sticker slogan. And those on the losing side of the ballot usually spend the next two to four years trying to scrape off the remnants of their loyalty. Number decals are the latest bumper sticker fad for racing fans. They not only indicate driver loyalty but also signal the growing popularity of stock car racing. And these stickers are seen not only on pickup truck bumpers. They're on windshields, truck cabs, lunch boxes, trailer hitches, and even ball caps and coffee mugs. Number by number, they make a public declaration: "This is the driver I'm for. When he's on the track, I'm rooting for him to win."

Likewise, dad, you carry your family's number onto the track every day. Wherever you go and whatever you do, you represent the home team.

- You represent their goals and dreams.
- You represent their skills and disciplines.
- You represent their strengths and weaknesses.

And all the while, you silently pray that your team will be proud of your behavior, proud to carry your number.

That's why you carefully mold your family. That's why you spend time honing your children's abilities. That's why you encourage their efforts, why you hurt when a child missteps and rejoice when one makes a winning decision.

In that sense, you are like the Apostle Paul of the New Testament fame. He dared to post his team's job description on the web site of his times—a public letter. He wrote of his team: "We are . . . Christ's ambassadors, as though God were making his appeal through us" (2 Corinthians 5:20).

That's you, dad. Represent your family well.

Dad the Crew Chief

Dad is the crew chief in the sense that he makes the team function at maximum capacity.

Clinical psychologist Wade Horn, former president of the

National Fatherhood Initiative, now a columnist for the *Washington Times,* put his finger on a critical issue for today's dads. He wrote:

> Today's culture seems to have become virtually obsessed with having fun. Instead of encouraging our young to develop self-restraint, MTV tells them, "A little lust, pride, sloth, and gluttony—in moderation—are fun, and that's what keeps your heart beating." In the same vein a California bumper sticker proclaims, "There is no right or wrong—only fun or boring." The consequences of this emphasis on having fun have been profound. Today, schools have become places where children expect—and demand—to be entertained. Parents, too, have come to believe their primary mission is to make sure their children are having a good time.[3]

Imagine NASCAR driver Jeff Green's crew chief saying something like this to his team during a yellow-flag pit stop, with fourteen laps to go in the Pepsi 400: "Guys, take your time out there. Just relax and enjoy the race. Set your own pace. We're just here to have a little fun."

Ludicrous!

That chief's job is to get seven crewmembers to function at maximum capacity in minimum time. The goal is not to "have a little fun," but to get the #30 car back on the track so the race car can finish first.

That's your job, too, Dad. You're not engaged in a popularity contest. Although parenting is a joy, you're not there just to have fun. You role is to provide for and equip your children so that they can be successful in life.

Fortunately, God has provided a few good tools for the job.

Dad Has a Few Good Tools

Let's call them the basic tools of a winning dad. These are the spiritual equivalent of your socket set, torque wrench, and pressure gauge—the mechanic's set for a great father.

Prayer

Paul Ward works in the engine shop of Richard Childress Racing. He says, "Putting God first has really helped my marriage. We pray every night and try to each morning. We never make any big decision without praying."[4] Paul discovered something far more important than the right fuel mix for a 700-horsepower engine. He discovered that prayer helps his family to function properly.

Daily time alone with God for prayer and Bible reading will do more to improve spiritual health than the proverbial apple a day that keeps the doctor away. And spiritual fitness is even more important than physical fitness. First Timothy 4:8, says, "Physical training is of some value, but godliness has value for all things, holding promise for both the present life and the life to come." The best way to keep a family in shape is to take it before the throne of God each day—by praying for family members by name.

If God's character is to be understood in terms of my life (as a father), what does my child think of God?

—Lee M. Haines

Instruction

NASCAR driver Hank Parker Jr. says of his support team, "A big help for me is my dad. We are the best of friends, and I can go to him with a question about the Bible . . . and he does his best to help me understand what it is I'm looking for."[5]

Dad, can you imagine your son coming to you and asking you how to play football—then sending him to Mom for instruction? That's unlikely. But something far more important than learning to throw an elliptical piece of pigskin is often passed off like a quarterback's lateral. We may teach our sons and daughters the basics of baseball and soccer but pass off giving spiritual instruction to someone else.

Ephesians 6:14 gives some fatherly advice: "Fathers, do not exasperate your children; instead, bring them up in the training and instruction of the Lord." Home is the best training camp for life. Dad, teach your kids about the faith. Teach them how to live, not just how to work and play.

Discipline

NASCAR driver Lake Speed was running 210 miles per hour at Talladega when the Lord said to him, "What next? You've won at all other types of racing, what are you going to do after you win in Winston Cup?"

That loving, inner rebuke was life changing for Speed. "When the Lord asked that question, I knew I had nowhere else to hide. Nothing else had worked up to this time—fame, money, success, and all the toys."[6] That jab in the conscience was just what he needed to make a major life change.

Proverbs 3:12 reminds us that "the Lord disciplines those he loves." Regardless of what you've heard lately, loving discipline is still an important part of family life. The dad who ignores little Susie when she throws herself on the floor and screams like a coyote with an ingrown toenail isn't being a responsible crew chief.

Child battering is a national tragedy and must never be excused. But a timely time-out never hurt anyone. The proverbial woodshed has been relegated to the Smithsonian Institution, but good fathers still refuse to allow their children to rule their own lives—or their households. Letting a child have his or her own way all the time prevents that child from learning to obey God. Fathers who lovingly and firmly set appropriate limits for their children's behavior will enable those children to succeed.

Love

Tad Geschickter, owner of the #59 Busch Series car, was raised in a Christian home. He had a good relationship with the Lord until he strayed during his young adult years. Then a business crisis forced him to re-examine his life. He wrote, "The amazing thing to me about the whole situation is that I had turned away from Christ and had become self reliant. But in an instant, when I turned back to Him—even though I didn't deserve it—He was there for me."[7]

Tad learned a lesson about God's love—His unfailing, redeeming, constant, forgiving love. That's the same love that heals broken families. It's the same love that lays pride aside and runs with open arms to embrace the guilty or the lonely. And it's the same love that builds strength and character in a young person.

If our children know that they are truly loved, then they are truly blessed.

Romans 13:8 says there is such a thing as a *good* debt, the debt of love. "Let no debt remain outstanding, except the continuing debt to love one another, for he who loves his fellowman has fulfilled the law." But you can't make payments on that account by direct deposit—the debt of love must be paid in person.

In the book *God has Never Failed Me, But He's Sure Scared Me to Death a Few Times*, the story is told of an orchard owner who recruited some boys to pick apples. A boy named Jimmy was chosen to be a sorter, since he seemed to be the best worker.

Trusting the new sorter, the owner went to town for some supplies. When he got back, he saw poor Jimmy sitting behind a mountain of fruit with one apple in each hand and a puzzled look on his face. "What in the world happened?" said the orchard owner.

"All these apples look the same to me," the boy said with a puzzled look on his face. "I can pick 'em, but I guess I just can't choose 'em."[8]

Winning dads don't do any picking and choosing. They love each of their family members equally—and completely. It's the basic duty of a dad.

Encouragement

Steve deSouza is vice president of operations for Joe Gibbs's Busch Series team. Once successful in powerboat racing, deSouza had to abandon that career because of a physical ailment. He reports, "Through prayer, God opened a door for me to get into auto racing with a group of guys that believe in prayer, men who are great mentors, and who live by faith in God."[9]

Men who are great mentors.

That's a great job description for dads: men who invest education, effort, and affirmation into the lives of others.

You know the old saying: "Behind every successful man . . . there is a mother with a thumb in his back!" That's not exactly the case. Closer to the truth is this: Behind every successful man there is someone *patting* him on the back.

It stands to reason that if we enjoy a pat on the back for a job well done, our children do too—more so, in fact. Remember that your kids don't have a track record. They're rookies in the game of life. Their successes today are their only successes so far. Give them the motivation they need to keep going. Praise them, and they'll try harder. Affirm them, and they'll pick themselves up after a fall. Encourage your kids to success.

You Can Do This!

After Dale Jarrett's come-from-behind win in the 2002 Pepsi 400 at Michigan International Speedway, his crew chief, Todd Parrott, was interviewed about the race. Parrott was quick to praise his driver, who had survived a spinout in the grass to race his way into victory lane. The chief also praised his crew for the way they put the #88 car back together and sent it onto the track again after the mishap.

But before that, he thanked God. And he added words that should stir every dad's soul: "I want to win the race of life." Then, proving that he was in the winner's circle for dads, he gave greetings to his wife and children, "I want to thank my family. They mean more to me than all of this."

Owner.

Driver.

Crew chief.

Dads have a lot of duties. Day after day, uptown or down on the farm, they're marking off the checklist and making a difference in the lives of their children.

The late and great humorist Erma Bombeck gave the world a fitting tribute to dads when she wrote of her husband's fatherly traits:

> He threw [his children] higher than his head until they were weak from laughter. He cast the deciding vote on the puppy debate. He listened more than he talked. He let them make mistakes. He allowed them to fall from their first two-wheeler without having a heart attack. He read a newspaper while they were trying to parallel park a car for the first time in preparation for their driving test.

Then she added a great bit of advice for any dad: "But mostly, a good father involves himself in his kid's lives. The more responsibility he has for a child, the harder it is to walk out of his life. A father has the potential to be a powerful force in the life of a child. Grab it!"[10]

Go for it, Dad. You can.

What Is a Dad?

A dad is a fella who tends a dream,
        from an armful to an embrace;
Who smiles at your very first tear,
Laughs at your very first tumble,
And then cries at the memory of both.

A dad is a fella who heals calamities
        with a kiss on the forehead,
Who tells you to play outside and
        then looks for you at every window,
Who pretends sleep past the curfew
        of your first date.

A Dad is a fella who whispers
        the wisdom of heaven into tiny ears,
And waits breathlessly for earthly echoes;
Who looks with moistened eyes
        into your very soul,
Who tiptoes to your room,
        tucks a woolen blanket under your chin
        and worships God.

                                    —Jerry Brecheisen

Openness is Key for David Smith

David Smith believes that honesty is the best policy when it comes to being a dad. The father of two boys, nineteen-year-old Joshua and seven-year-old Justin, says he and his wife, Karen, taught their boys early on that they could come to their parents with questions. "I let them know they can talk to me," David says. Calling their boys "a blessing," the Smiths brought them up in a Bible-believing church and taught them at an early age about the Christian faith. He advises, "Be honest with your children and tell them every day that you love them." And the pit boss is not above showing affection. "Hug them a lot," David says, "the time you have with them is precious."

Winning Dad Tip

Always keep the line of communication open.

*Winning dads
maintain a healthy
spiritual life.*

High Performance Hearts
Maintaining Your Spiritual Life

 *I make sure that I'm in the Scriptures on a regular basis. I'm also in an accountability group with eight other members of the Joe Gibbs racing team. Along with that, I have a time of daily prayer and make sure my family and I are plugged into a local church.*

—Jeff Chandler, NASCAR Mechanic
Tony Stewart's #20 Car

Racing engines push the limits of performance. It takes a highly tuned engine to turn more than 9,000 RPMs and produce up to 750 horsepower. One racing engineer put it this way: "A high performance race engine, by its definition, indicates that limits are going to be pushed. The limit that is of most concern, as far as pistons are concerned, is peak operating cylinder pressure. Maximizing cylinder pressure benefits horsepower and fuel economy."[1]

Would you agree that we live in a limits-pushing age? Any man who thinks he can lead the field on a moped in this high-stress world will sooner or later be flattened by a Mercedes! You'll need a high-performance heart to finish first with your family. That may require some spiritual adjustments.

How to Tune up Your Heart

The right fuel mix.

Reduced lift.

Fresh tires.

An engine adjustment.

In racing, fine-tuning often makes the difference between reaching the finish line and the *finished* line. What's true on the track is true at home—dads need to keep their spiritual lives in perfect adjustment.

How do you do that?

Let's take some advice from the veterans—those who've actually turned a few laps. Here are some tips from the pros on how to live for Christ in a world that's running at a redline pace.

Focus on the Future

First, focus on the future. Look through the windshield more than the mirrors. Certainly, an occasional glimpse in the mirror could mean the difference between carving prime rib at a victory dinner and opening the cellophane wrapper on some saltine crackers from a hospital bed—with loose teeth. But those who finish first focus on this lap, not the last one. They spend more time looking ahead than back.

A New Testament veteran gave this worthy example, "Forgetting what is behind and straining toward what is ahead, I press on toward the goal to win the prize for which God has called me heavenward in Christ Jesus" (Philippians 3:13–14). The Apostle Paul knew that ultimate victory belongs to the *faithful* not the *fretful*. Throwing pity parties for past mistakes only spins your wheels. Don't look in the rearview mirror of *coulda–shoulda–if only.*

"I could have . . . if only . . ."

"I should have . . . but . . ."

If you want a high performance heart, focus on the future. When your past is forgiven, it's forgotten. Jesus is a futurist not a historian. First John 1:9 promises us a clean slate: "If we confess our sins, he is faithful and just and will forgive us our sins and purify us from all unrighteousness."

God never gives closed-door "loser lectures" in the garage. He didn't conquer the Cross only to leave us limping back to pit road with a blown engine and a bad attitude. He made us victors!

Bruce Wilkinson learned a valuable lesson about God's encouragement while taking a trip to the park with his family. One of his sons climbed the ladder of a middle-sized slide on the park playground. Conquering the medium slide, he proceeded to the larger—giving Mom an anxious moment. The boy started up the ladder, then stopped. His inclination to descend was overruled by the presence of a teenager behind him.

Panic.

Then Dad rushed in to calm his fears, and the boy asked his father to go down the slide with him.

Wilkinson recalls, "I stretched as high as I could to reach him and lifted him into my arms. Then we climbed that long ladder up the clouds together. At the top, I put my son between my legs and wrapped my arms around him. Then we went zipping down the slide together, laughing all the way. That is what your Father's hand is like. You tell Him, 'Father, please do this in me because I can't do it alone! It's too big for me!' And you step out in faith to do and say things that could only come from His hand."[2]

God wants to give you a hand. He wants to wrap His arms around you and zip through life together—laughing all the way.

It won't be *all* laughs, of course. There will be a few fender benders, and even some head-jarring, liver-rearranging wall bangers. But when God rides with you, you get the help you need to overcome any setback. Jesus said, "Remain in me, and I will remain in you. No branch can bear fruit by itself; it must remain in the vine. Neither can you bear fruit unless you remain in me. 'I am the vine; you are the branches. If a man remains in me and I in him, he will bear much fruit; apart from me you can do nothing'" (John 15:4–5).

Did you get that? Remain in Him, and the future is an open book.

NASCAR driver Randy Tolsma reminds us about the resource of real faith, "Keep an open mind to who God is. It's not about rules and laws, it's a relationship."[3]

Keep looking to your future. God is.

Give Yourself Away

We like to hoard things. When we get a little money, status, power, or affirmation, we usually keep it for ourselves. But winners—on the track and in the home—realize that you gain most by giving. That's another secret for keeping your spiritual life in top shape. Be more concerned with your *output* than with your *intake*. Be willing to give yourself away.

It's funny that those who reach the top often forget whose shoulders carried them there. But NASCAR fans aren't stingy when it comes to supporting their sport.

Top Ten Ways to Spot a NASCAR Fan

10. At least one of his children is named after a racetrack.

9. He wears earplugs and sunglasses at the symphony.

8. He's taken a cooler to church.

7. He has a signed undershirt.

6. His doorbell chimes play "I'm Proud to be an American."

5. He's taken 500 laps past a fast food drive-up window.

4. His romantic evenings include videos of Michigan International Speedway.

3. He has a driver number on the back of his pajamas.

2. His bird dog only points when it sees an eagle decal.

1. He has more caps than a movie star's teeth.

—Jerry Brecheisen

Some Jesus fans in the early days of the church had a handle on giving. Here's the record of their generosity:

Brothers, we want you to know about the grace that God

has given the Macedonian churches. Out of the most severe trial, their overflowing joy and their extreme poverty welled up in rich generosity. For I testify that they gave as much as they were able, and even beyond their ability. Entirely on their own, they urgently pleaded with us for the privilege of sharing in this service to the saints. And they did not do as we expected, but they gave themselves first to the Lord and then to us in keeping with God's will (2 Corinthians 8:1–5).

What a group! Religious terrorists had plundered their homes. The times were tougher than a ten-day-old Krispy Kreme. Things were so bad that they'd have needed a bank loan to buy a sausage biscuit. But when they heard about the financial setback of their Christian brothers and sisters in Jerusalem, they determined to help.

They had high performance hearts.

Where does that leave us—we who swipe our plastic for silver and gold? It leaves us with a decision. Will we live our lives as if other people didn't exist? Will we spend our time tearing down our houses to build newer, bigger ones, like the rich fool in Jesus' stirring story? (See Luke 12:13–21.) Or will we build basic shelters for the homeless?

A "getting" heart is bloated and uncomfortable. A giving heart is contented and peaceful. Pride and luxury are the vices of an also-ran. Generosity is the mark of a winner—at work, at home, and everywhere in life.

Give yourself away, Dad. Give your money, your time, and your attention to those who need it. Use your life to build others.

Guard Your Eyes

The best looking race car doesn't always win. What's under the hood matters more than what's on the skin. Performance counts more than a flashy paint job. You've probably wasted at least one paycheck on a used Chevy that looked better than it ran, so you know that appearances can be deceiving.

Remember that, Dad, when your eyes want to wander. Don't be misled by appearance.

In our Ken-and-Barbie world, the Madison Avenue mavens know that "sex sells." But it's also a buyer! Love-less, vow-less sex always takes; it never gives the intimacy that it promises. It is void of God's original intent for human sexual fulfillment.

Passionate love in the bedroom of marriage is God's plan. You'll never find that on an Internet sex site or in an after-work romance.

That's why high performance hearts steer clear of alluring looks and inviting glances. Winning dads have made a deal with their eyes—they refuse to look at images that have only a sexual intent. They say no when others say yes.

That kind of moral strength doesn't come from a discount power bar at the Vitamins-R-Us store. It comes from God.

The Apostle Paul said that "if the Spirit of him who raised Jesus from the dead is living in you, he who raised Christ from the dead will also give life to your mortal bodies through his Spirit, who lives in you" (Romans 8:11).

That's spiritual power with no restrictor plates—raise-from-the-dead, conquer-the-world, change-the-heart spiritual power.

God has the power to help you live in digital color in a world of monochrome morality. The Bible tells us: "Holiness characterizes God. And that holiness must be reflected in His people. 'It is written: Be holy, because I am holy' (1 Peter 1:16). It seems implausible. You mean we can reflect God's holiness?

Yes, we can.

The heavenly Father invites us to be like Him. That impossible dream becomes a reality when we surrender our lives to the power and control of His Holy Spirit. "The impossible becomes possible through the provisions of His Son, Jesus Christ, and the power of His Holy Spirit."[4]

Your buddies may say, "If it feels good, do it." But just because something feels good does not mean that it is good. One feel-good decision in an out-of-bounds area could affect your entire life—and your family!

God has made inner strength available to you—enough to send back the world's RSVPs with a "Thanks, but no thanks."

The decisions that affect your behavior begin in the mind. Motivational speaker Dr. Peter Hirsch says we need to listen to the inner voice. "There are some people you just don't want in your home—right? So you don't let them in. Or if they're already inside, you ask them to leave. It's the same thing with thoughts. Kick the thoughts you don't want out of your mind. Like a diplomat or like a six-foot-six bouncer—it's up to you. Just make sure the unwanted thoughts are gone! Your mind is your castle. It's up to you to have around the kind of thoughts you want to hang around with."[5]

Value Relationships over Money

To keep your spiritual life fired up, focus more on your bonds than your stocks. That is, value relationships more than money.

Top-ten drivers aren't concerned only with tire wear and

engine performance. They also have to be concerned about the management of millions of dollars. Having the right CPA is almost as important as getting the right RPMs. These days, the rise in interest rates affects a racing team nearly as much as the bank of the track.

Yet wives, children, siblings, and parents are not listed on the stock market. Why? Because their worth is beyond measure. The people in your life are far more important than any financial port-folio. Your investment in people will pay greater dividends than any 401K.

Right now, money—or the lack of it—may seem to dominate your life. You're pressed by the need to make a mortgage pay-ment, replace the muffler, sock away a few bucks for retirement, and, oh yeah, buy some groceries. But don't allow the urgent need for capital to cloud your view of the eternal. As you earn a living, remember that living is the goal.

Pass up the overtime now and then so you can show up at a recital. Spend some of those hard-earned vacation days on a fam-ily camping trip. Provide your family with a home, not just a big house. Give them something they need far more than money—your time and attention.

Fifty years from now, mutual respect will be worth more than your mutual funds. The fact that you have a lot of cash won't matter if you've cashed in all your chances to be a dad.

NASCAR driver Robert Pressley puts money in exactly the right position on the priority list. He said, "Jesus Christ and my family are the most important things in my life. Everything else comes after that."[6]

> *The most important thing a father can do*
> *for his children is to love their mother.*
>
> —Theodore Hesburgh

Keep the Faith

Occasionally, a mighty racing machine may be seen at the close of a great race putting along like a pachyderm with a sprained ankle. The pole sitter winds up pooped. Why? He ran out of fuel.

Somebody calculated wrong.

The driver stayed on the throttle too long.

The team tried to skip one pit stop.

They did everything they could to win—but they forgot to check the fuel. As a result, the racer fell from the lead on the very last lap, watching in agonized slow-motion as every driver in the field raced past.

A lot of life's pole sitters have finished the same way:

- They lacked the commitment to finish a marriage.
- They ran out of faith in a crisis.
- Their character didn't have the right mix of courage and determination.
- They ran too hard for too long, neglecting the spiritual life.

The Apostle Paul made a winning personal commitment at a critical moment in his life. He said, "And now, compelled by the Spirit, I am going to Jerusalem, not knowing what will happen to me there. I only know that in every city the Holy Spirit warns me that prison and hardships are facing me. However, I consider my life worth nothing to me, if only I may finish the race and complete the task the Lord Jesus has given me—the task of testifying to the gospel of God's grace" (Acts 20:22–24).

"The winner and still champion!"

Paul was determined to finish the race. He committed all of his energy to a single goal: to honor God.

Winning dads do the same. They commit their entire lives—body, mind, and spirit—to completing the God-given task of being a father.

In racing, points champions don't win trophies accidentally. They plan to win. They calculate the resources that are necessary to finish the season. Theirs is a world of laptops, stopwatches, and gauges. They understand what will be required of them if they are to win, and they make the commitment to go all the way.

Winning dads make a similar calculation—

- They plan time for daily prayer and the study of God's Word.
- They spend more time with family than with friends.
- They avoid going to places that will put their faith in jeopardy.
- They bring their children to church.
- They keep a lid on lust.
- They learn to manage stress and anger.
- They pay attention to their physical health.
- They spend money wisely.

It's a long season, Dad. Make the right decisions with your time, money, and attention and you'll be a faithful father for years to come.

Run in Front

During a NASCAR race, you'll notice some drivers that are running very well. Their cars are as fast as their competitors. They have plenty of fuel. They're running on fresh tires. They have the right combination of machinery and manpower to finish the race. There's only one problem: they're a lap behind!

Do everything you can to stay on the winning lap.

A local reporter asked Dale Jarrett about his plans for the 2002 IROC race at the Brickyard. Jarrett explained that he had made a few discoveries during the previous day's practice. The veteran driver noted that it was difficult to pass if you were running behind someone. He said that the car performs better if it's out in front.

Race cars need "clean air." It's the same with Christian dads!

Isaiah was an Old Testament prophet who served as God's spokesman. He gave the formula for keeping your spiritual life on track when he said:

> Wash and make yourselves clean. Take your evil deeds out of my sight! Stop doing wrong, learn to do right! Seek justice, encourage the oppressed. Defend the cause of the fatherless, plead the case of the widow. "Come now, let us reason together," says the Lord. "Though your sins are like scarlet, they shall be as white as snow; though they are red as crimson, they shall be like wool. If you are willing and obedient, you will eat the best from the land; but if you resist and rebel, you will be devoured by the sword." For the mouth of the Lord has spoken (Isaiah 1:16–20).

Stay on the lead lap with God. When you sin, confess it quickly. If you spot a spiritual problem, address it immediately.

Small sins, little bits of disobedience, some anger, minor indiscretions—these are "bad air" for a Christian father. If you allow them to remain in your life they'll only hinder your spiritual growth.

There's something more important than taking a 3,000–pound stock car to the finish line, and that's finishing the race as a successful husband and father. To do that, you'll need to keep your heart in racing tune. Commit yourself to God. Make the choices that contribute to your spiritual growth. Resist the temptations of the enemy. Keep your heart in tune and you'll run first with your family all day long.

Smiles are Important for Randy Tolsma

NASCAR driver Randy Tolsma says even a smile is important to being a good dad. Randy and his wife Tiffanie are the parents of an infant son, Elijah. Randy not only shared in preparing for the arrival of his son but also made a commitment to spend time with him. "I determined to give him unconditional love," Randy says. He expresses affection for Elijah with a hug and says, "I always make sure he gets a smile." Randy and Tiffanie are dedicated Christians who are determined to raise their child in an environment that reflects their joyful faith in the Lord Jesus Christ.

Winning Dad Tip

Show your children that you love them.

Winning dads
know what's
important.

Pole Position
Putting First Things First

It wasn't till Jesus got hold of me that I knew
what life was all about. Now I live in the fullness
of what God has for those who seek Him.

—David Smith, Pit Crew Manager
Richard Childress Racing

Every driver wants to start the race at the pole. As practice and qualifying laps are run, drivers, owners, and crewmembers anxiously watch the scoring pylon to see who will win the coveted pole position. That driver, starting the race on the inside position of the front row, enjoys an obvious advantage over the rest of the field. It helps to start in front!

Focus is as essential to racing as a ripcord on a parachute. Not everyone who drags a pit box and driver helmet to Daytona will win a spot on the starting grid. Only those teams who have the right priorities will make the race—and only one of them will win the pole.

It's the same in life. Priorities form the foundation for personal achievement. People who succeed are those who have learned to put first things first. A race driver might get to victory lane by taking a wrong turn out of the garage—but he won't stay long! Victory lane is reserved for the driver who keeps his car running in spite of all obstacles and finishes ahead of the pack.

That requires a tremendous dedication to win and a clear focus on the essentials of running a race.

Focus is important for dads too. There are four areas of life that must function well for a father to be successful. Think of them as the engine, chassis, suspension, and steering on a car—when they're working well, the car runs beautifully. They are spirit, body, emotions, and family. The dad that puts first things first in these areas of life will be a success with his family.

Set Spiritual Priorities

Although he's been a Christian since 1983, veteran driver Darrell Waltrip admits that he didn't always have the right priorities. Then he made an important discovery: "As I began to grow as a Christian, I began to realize that there were things in life more important than winning races. . . . I began to see that serving God needed to be first."[1]

That priority affects all the rest.

Worship

Every other area of your life may be running on eight cylinders, but if there's sludge in your spiritual life, you're not going to finish. Although spirituality is the most essential component of our lives, it may be the easiest to ignore. When we're pushed in a thousand directions, worship is the easiest thing to drop from the schedule.

But we were created to have fellowship with God, and without that fellowship there will always be hole in our hearts.

According to Norman G. Wilson, "Our search for righteousness (spiritual right-ness) cannot be a casual afterthought or hobby; it must be a way of life. Like the hunger pangs that make us desperate for food and the parched throat that makes us long for water, our souls must have a deep desire—a craving—for God."[2]

What's the first priority in your life? If it's something other than knowing God, reshuffle the pack and try again.

Trust

The doctor emerged from the examining room to speak confidentially with the wife of his patient.

"Mrs. Smith, I'm a bit concerned about your husband's condition," he said.

"I am too," the wife replied, "I've tried to get him to spend more time on that treadmill, but you know how he likes cheesecake!"

"No, I'm afraid you misunderstood me," the doctor continued. "I'm concerned that he is losing some ground."

"Oh that!" the wife explained. "Don't worry about that. We've got the same two acres we had when we first moved here. If you mean those white flags in the yard, it's to mark the invisible fence for our Chihuahua. We've had her on hormone therapy, and last week she got out and bit the leg off our neighbor's pit bull."

Do you feel like you're losing ground? Don't!

God has provided enough resources for you to overcome every obstacle in life. From the forgiveness of your past to faith for your future, God's guarantees are never revised.

Second Corinthians 9:8 spells out the terms of an astonishing "manufacturer's warranty." "God is able to make all grace abound to you, so that in all things at all times, having all that you need, you will abound in every good work." *All* is a rather inclusive word. It means that every ounce of God's resources is available to meet your need.

Confession

Winning dads understand the importance of a spiritual tune-up. They know that when they're out of sorts with God, they're usually out of sorts with everyone else. NASCAR driver Robert Pressley said, "As I became a teenager I started to stray away from the Lord. I wasn't that bad, just doing those things most teenage boys do, but I knew that I was wrong and nothing I could do could block out my knowledge of my sins."[3]

Are you out of sorts, Dad? Just like Pressley, you can arrange a meeting with the ultimate owner—God. Present your fears or failures to Him in a spirit of repentance ("I'm sorry, enough to make a U-turn") and then take what's coming—forgiveness.

Keep God first in your life. You'll be a better dad—and a happier person—for it.

God warms his hands at man's heart when he prays.

—John Masefield

Set Physical Priorities

Most often, the way we feel affects the way we act. And "feel-bad" behavior often results from neglecting physical health. If the body is a temple (and it is), then some folk probably need an estimate for new aluminum siding! These specimens of neglect are content to strap themselves into a recliner and yell for room service. They get their exercise draining the batteries on the remote control as they alternate between the all-news and all-sports channels on the wide-screen television. Their advanced regimen consists of prying the top off a Pringles can.

Others are like veteran driver Mark Martin, who is known for being in the weight room before breakfast, pumping iron to make sure his body is as fit as his race car. Martin knows that physical fitness affects racing finesse. That's true also for those who *don't* make their living by chasing friends around a two-mile oval.

Would you like to set some physical priorities?

Diet

First, watch your table settings. Good health begins at the breakfast bar—and continues at the lunch counter and dinner table. Eating right means making choices based on health and nutrition, not taste alone. It takes only a minimum daily requirement of wisdom to see that a "fruit group" isn't two raspberry sodas, and a corn dog isn't a vegetable.

The wise choices are worth it. Improving your health will improve your self-image. And a dad's good self-image has a positive effect on his family.

Exercise

Each day, exercise your option to engage in some physical activity. Regular physical exercise—whether it's a twenty-minute walk or a two-hour workout—will benefit every area of your life, including soul, mind, and family. Family? Yes! Exercise is a great stress reliever. When dad is relaxed the whole family breathes easier.

Leadership expert John Maxwell said, "You will never change your life until you change something you do daily. The secret of your success is found in your daily routine."[4]

Rest

You might think the most important thing you can do for your family is to earn more money. In fact, it could be to get more sleep. To do that, you may have to let Letterman and Leno entertain themselves. Leave the late show early and go to bed.

For many dads, the classic T-shirt slogan has a ring of truth, "Sometimes I wake up grumpy . . . and sometimes I let him sleep." Getting a good night's rest will improve your health—and your attitude. It's true that for some, getting eight hours' sleep is as probable as teaching a snake to roller skate, especially if your newborn is doing mommy calls at 2 A.M. But rest is important to your health and your family. Get some.

Set Emotional Priorities

NASCAR driver Jason Keller said, "With all the traveling and all the different paths in life that you can take, I needed something to hold onto, something that didn't change. And I knew that God was the one thing in life that was stable. He never changes."[5]

But we do.

Our feelings can be as fickle as a mallard duck in a Miami hurricane. We are emotional beings, and we have honest-to-goodness feelings that are affected by our surroundings.

Triggered by external factors, we may weep or laugh, rejoice or grieve. Our feelings are subject to natural highs and lows. Jason Keller said, "In this sport there are so many ups and downs! One week you're on top of the world and the next you can be in the wall!"[6]

So what's the strategy? How can we keep from getting sideways in a world that's out of whack?

Hobbies

Diversity is good not only for your financial portfolio but also for your emotional portfolio. Every dad needs some stress busters, pleasant diversions from the daily grind. One of the best is a good hobby.

One NASCAR driver was asked what he did before a very important practice. The reporter probably waited to hear about some intense "focus ritual" like squeezing a Pepsi can until the pull tab pops. But the driver surprised him with this calm report of his morning's activity: "I went fishing."

Doing something out of the ordinary usually relieves stress. Take a break from your nine-to-five by hitting the links, hitting a nail on the head, or hitting a flea market. That break from the ordinary will be a hit with your body and soul. It will also be a hit with your family. They'll appreciate having a dad who is emotionally at ease.

Unless your good hobby becomes a bad habit, that is!

You'll know the difference, and so will your wife. When you start wearing your golf shoes to bed, it's time to skip your next tee time. When the kids have to make an appointment for a good-night kiss between your poetry class and your bowling league, your diversity has become a disaster.

Get a hobby, and pursue it appropriately. It'll boost your spirits.

Solitude

Peace and quiet is not the name of a law firm. It's a finish-line strategy for twenty-first century dads. Solitude is an important safeguard for emotional health. Sometimes the best thing you can do for yourself (and your family) is nothing. A Psalm writer advised, "Be still before the Lord and wait patiently for him; do not fret when men succeed in their ways, when they carry out their wicked schemes" (Psalm 37:7). Try it.

- Get up a few minutes early to sit on the deck and listen to nature's surround sound.
- Turn off the infomercial offering "exclusive" weight-loss programs and listen to the quiet.
- Drive to work without the FM foolishness of a drive-time DJ. Use the time to reflect on God's presence.
- Plan a vacation that doesn't include making the *Guinness Book of World Records* for most miles driven in one week.
- Find a garden place at home or at work where you can be alone to read, reflect, and pray.

The world is a tough place. Your emotions need time to heal after being dragged through the daily grind. Stop. Look. Listen. The mind you save may be your own!

Set Family Priorities

Grief is what taught NASCAR driver Joe Nemechek the value of family. It wasn't until after his brother died that he discovered the need to make family relationships a priority. Joe said:

> I lost a brother a few years ago, and he was my best friend. It has been one of the hardest things I have ever had to go through. You know that we take a lot of things for granted. I used to see my brother almost every day. I called him that morning to tell him Happy Birthday, and didn't think anything about it. You know we go racing and go back home, never thinking anything is going to change. But when that happened, it made me think of what I took for granted.[7]

The spouse, children, parents, and siblings that God has put on your team were chosen before time. But their care and keeping must be on your daily checklist.

It's easy to spot a dad who has *not* made his family a priority. At a restaurant, he'll be the guy sipping soda while his wife is trying to keep the two-year-old from eating the salt shaker, running relays to the restroom with the twins, and making a panicky effort to prevent a homicide between two teenagers.

Where's Pop?

He's probably browsing the menu and whining because they're isn't enough ice in his glass!

Winning dads make family a priority. Here's how.

Provision

NASCAR driver Lake Speed reflected, "Most of my life I had all the things the world says will make you happy, the big house, the cars and boat, and I had also been very successful. But there was still an emptiness inside."[8] Lake learned something that every billionaire already knows: money isn't everything.

Yet a dad's priority is to provide for his family, and that does include providing income.

Finances. No matter how many family members work outside the home, dad has a supervisory responsibility for "the meeting of the ends." He is responsible for setting the financial agenda—or at least serving as co-chairperson along with mom—of the home's "finance committee." An attentive father will spot dangerous trends and make course corrections—

- If the store clerk has to use a magnifying glass to read the worn-out numbers on the credit card, then it's time to pay cash.
- If the family's piggy bank is asthmatic from the dust that has settled on it, it's time to switch from *cravings* to *savings.*
- If more than one family member is working overtime to make payments on the boat, it's time to board up the third door of the three-car garage.

A good father can say no to a "good deal" when it doesn't fit the family budget.

Stability. Fathers provide more than finances. They provide security as well. Families look to dad as the rock. He provides the "it'll-be-all-right" factor, that positive attitude which is an anchor for the storms of a post–nine-eleven world.

There's a classic story of a little boy who was sitting in the coach section of an airplane. In midflight, a storm began to shake the plane like a puppy with a knotted sock. One of the adult passengers looked at the boy and remarked, "Son, aren't you a little bit nervous?"

"Nope!" the boy replied confidently.

"Why not?" the passenger inquired.

"My Dad's flying this thing. And this is his regular route."

When dad is on the scene, the family can relax. Be there, Dad. Your family is counting on you.

Affirmation. NASCAR driver Hank Parker Jr. says, "There is a lot of pressure out there, and it helps to surround yourself with people who will help build you up and not tear you down."[9] Dads are not just the enforcers of the family, they're also the affirmers.

An Olympic bobsled gold medallist was asked about his job during a TV news program. "I'm a pusher," he remarked. "I'm a pusher athlete." His role was to give the bobsled a starting push. That's a good job description for a dad: a pusher athlete. Good fathers give the family a boost. They encourage their children to try new things by affirming their abilities. They set the stage for success by praising their kids' achievements. An affirming father sets a positive tone for his child's entire life. Saying "I believe in you," with or without words, will cause a child to believe in him- or herself.

Affection. Dads also provide affection for their families. They make them feel secure by openly expressing their love for them. Many a child's inner war has been won with a hug or kiss. The three little words that turn houses into homes aren't "What's for supper?" They are "I love you," and a loving dad will speak them often.

When was the last time you told your sweetheart that you loved her? Have your kids heard that you love them—from you?

Say it today.

Instruction. Veteran driver Dale Jarrett credits the influence of a mentor, Joe Gibbs, for the positive changes in his life. "Things started changing when I started driving for Joe Gibbs," Jarrett said. "Here was a man that is very strong in the Lord, and his influence on me helped me get my life back to where it should be. My wife and I dedicated our lives to the Lord, and we know that our children are growing up in a Christian home."[10]

Dads don't teach with presentations in PowerPoint or line drawings on a chalkboard. Their instruction is displayed in their lives—like a logo on the uniform of a NASCAR driver. They teach by example as well as with their words. They give object lessons in faith, character, discipline, and relationships.

In one sense, dads are pastors also, although they don't usually have a pulpit. And just like vocational pastors, their congregations sometimes fall asleep during the sermon! But they have a congregation of at least one, from toddler to teen. Their "parishioners" put their feet under the same table where the "pastor" eats microwave dinners. That makes it doubly important for every father to practice what he preaches. Children learn by example.

Protection

A father's ultimate priority is to protect his family. That means creating an atmosphere of safety at home. Paul Ward of Richard Childress Racing's engine shop said, "Here at the shop, Richard and all the managers are really supportive of us having a weekly prayer and Bible study, and it has made a big difference."[11]

Creating a safe environment at home is not as simple as it used to be. There was a time when all the big bad wolves were in nursery rhymes. Now they have E-mail addresses and stroll through the ethereal avenues of the Internet. Dads need to be on a heightened state of alert. There really are monsters out there!

That means that the role of a father has changed. Now, a father has to keep watch on the television, the Internet, the mall, and the MP3 player. One thing hasn't changed, however. Dad is still the point man for protecting his family.

From Harmful Attitudes. The culture you live in is trying to convince your family that "anything goes." In this permissive world, you'll need to teach them a painful little word—*No.*

Start early. By the time Jimmy or Judy has reached the freshman dorm, it'll be too late. Toddlerville is a good a place to put up speed-limit signs. Even tykes on tricycles need to know there are some no passing zones. And they need to know that they won't always get by with a "warning" when they break the law.

From Harmful Addictions. No, you can't be behind every barn, making sure that the little ones aren't lighting this or drinking that. But you can set an example with your own life. You can refuse to use addictive substances, and you can teach your family about their dangers. If you don't, who will?

From Harmful Affiliations. There's an old adage that goes something like this: Say no to their friends and soon they'll be family. During the teen years, you'll need a double dose of wisdom. You'll need to know how to look beyond the pierced eyebrow of your son's date into her visionary gaze. You'll need to see beyond the lounge lizard look of your daughter's boyfriend into his soul.

You can't buy that kind of vision at a one-hour eyeglass shop. It will have to come from God. Fortunately, His wisdom is always in stock. James 1:3 says, "If any of you lacks wisdom, he should ask God, who gives generously to all without finding fault, and it will be given to him."

So ask.

God has promised to give you the right words at the right time—wisdom to love without giving license, to say enough without saying too much, to let go without going too far. You can't do this alone, and you weren't meant to. Ask your Father for advice. It's free.

You Can Win

Twenty-first-century parenting is like speed walking on a tightrope—with one eye shut! But you can do it. Many have, and have graduated with flying colors. (Black and blue?)

Here's the good news: you'll make it too! Set the right priorities. Trust your heavenly Father. Make heaven the first number on your speed dial—and call often.

Be faithful.

Be firm.

Be flexible.

Be funny.

And most important, be around.

Make your family your first priority, and before long you'll see yourself grinning in your son's wedding album—or crying in your daughter's! Either way, you'll be a winning dad.

Randy MacDonald Says Pass The Faith Along

Career Highlights

- 1984 NASCAR North Rookie of the Year
- 1990 Champion, GM National Stock Car Series
- 1993 Rookie of the Year in ASA AC-Delco Challenge Series

NASCAR driver Randy MacDonald is concerned about the next generation. Citing the influence of his parents on his own walk with the Lord, Randy says, "I want to pass my own faith along to my daughters, Jeni and Mackenzie." Randy and his wife Ginna not only take their children to an organized Bible study, they have devotional times as a family. Randy says, "It's important to teach children how to pray, but it's also important that they learn how to be thankful for answered prayer." During their family prayer time, the MacDonalds ask God for specific requests and then track answers to prayer on note cards. As a result, Jeni and Mackenzie see firsthand how God is at work in their lives.

Winning Dad Tip

Let your children see you pray.

*Winning dads
understand the
stages of a
child's life.*

Going the Distance
The Cycles of Parenting and Grandparenting

I didn't seem to have the time to go to church when I was younger because I was so involved in racing. But now I can't do without the Lord. . . . My desire is to give back to the Lord what He has done for me.

—Jeff Green, 2000 Busch Series Champion

The worst thing about being a parent is that by the time you get a handle on it, it's not your turn! In a way, being a father to little Matt or Mandi is like driving a race car: the guy on the track needs a lot of advice, but he's going in circles too fast to stop for directions. And it's the same in both racing and parenting: the "experts" watching from the stands always seem to know more than the driver.

Dad, the gap between your first race and your retirement to the broadcast booth is narrower than you can imagine. James 4:14 asks a pointed question: "What is your life? You are a mist that appears for a little while and then vanishes." Your threescore and ten years are nanoseconds compared to eternity. Days filled with diaper changes, doctor visits, and drama practices seem long, but they're the shortest and most important days of your life. In just eighteen or so years, you must pour the wisdom of the ages into minds that have a disturbing tendency to leak.

It's hard telling where you are in this race against time, so let's take a look at some of the laps you'll run, the cycles of being a dad or granddad.

Lap One: The Unsettled Years

Fortunately, most dads are young when their kids are. Later, you'll wonder how you ever made it through these unsettled years. They start the moment the doctor's office calls back with positive pregnancy test results.

Blue Flag: Giving Way to Mom's Needs

The moment that call comes, everything changes! A smorgasbord of emotions is being served in mom's mind, and dad is trying to "wait tables."

"How are you feeling, honey?"

"You have to ask?"

Suddenly, dad is on the front lines of the war on hormones. And for the next eight or nine months, the hormones will win! In racing, the blue flag with a diagonal yellow stripe is a signal for a driver to move over and let a faster car pass. During a wife's pregnancy, the dad who obeys the "move over flag" and gives way to his partner's needs will have an easier ride. Compare that to the holdout dad who insists on having his own way regardless of the changes taking place in his wife's mind and body. A fellow with that kind of judgement would probably make a right turn at Daytona!

Glorious months of mincing words and eating crow are in store for dad. He'll learn to comment on his wife's *glow* instead of her *girth* and happily make late-night trips to a "convenience" store for Moon Pies and RC Cola.

Then, just as dad thinks he's made it through the pregnancy, the birth happens.

Green Flag: Welcoming a New Life

The beginning of life is an awesome moment. It's also a challenge for a father. Most fathers face the moment well. Their names are inscribed on the winner's trophy. Others are scrawled in grease on the garage floor!

What makes a winning dad at the moment of birth? Here are a few marks of a champion.

Gratitude. Winning dads are grateful for the gift of life, and they know where it came from. They give thanks to God for the child that has been placed in their care.

Begin your child's life with a worship service. God has placed this unbelievably intricate bundle of nerves and skin and bone into your hands. You have been given the maintenance contract on a miracle. Be grateful for the opportunity.

Why, even the birth process is a miracle:

"Tiny, tadpole-like sperm battle the crashing currents of adversity in a furious freestyle swim toward a miniscule egg that God formed in His heart eons before He counted the brown particles of Sahara sand. A miraculous union culminates in a unique cell that splits into equally unique parts. And after approximately thirty-nine weeks of divine supervision and care, a tiny form pushes the *down* button on a psychological and physiological elevator, through a birth canal so small that its tiny skull has to cave in to make the journey, into the God-trained arms of an attendant. A child, formed with greater tenderness than the petal of a carnation, is born."[1]

After you've caught your breath, give thanks for the privilege of being a father.

Humility. New fathers must accept an uncomfortable position: second place. Mom didn't go through nine months of emotional chaos, nausea, cucumber sandwiches, and extra-large clothes in order to be there for you. She needs to concentrate her attention on her newborn. Your needs are the same as they were pre-pregnancy, but nobody is going to notice it for awhile!

Learn to live with it. You won't see many checkered flags, but as in NASCAR racing, second place pays pretty well for dads too!

First smiles.

First words.

First steps.

That tiny grip on your finger is a bonus check that beats any winner's trophy. So go with the flow, dad. Your wife and child need you right where you are.

What a wild ride it will be!

- Baby noises filling sleepless nights.
- Cell phone calls from the formula aisle of the supermarket.
- Fevers.
- Rashes.
- Green diapers.
- Worried trips to the doctor's office.
- Mommy-calming.

There are good things too. You have the opportunity to love a child absolutely. Your affirmation will make a boy or girl feel totally accepted. You have the privilege of holding seven or eight pounds of wonder in your arms and shower his or her mom with approval and affection.

Too soon, the time will pass. By the time dad learns how to live on a hundred and twenty minutes of sleep per night, baby will have learned how to sleep till dawn. Then it's time to turn the wheel.

Turns One and Two: Toddler Years

Welcome to high-banked, hazardous, crowded, confusing turn two. These are the toddler years.

These will be the times that try dad's soul. As junior grows, you'll notice that only half of his genes are yours. The rest come from your mother-in-law. At some point, every bad trait he has will rear its ugly head during a single mealtime—one food-throwing, milk-spilling, spoon-tossing, bib-smearing mealtime.

Bring it on! The dad who determines to make it past turn two usually does well for the entire race. And winning dads can make it with a smile on their face! Here are some tips for keeping in the groove on turn two.

Discipline. Winning dads can speak with a forked-tongue. They can say "no" and "I love you" at the same time. They know how to mix firmness with affirmation. They understand that from the seeds of these "terrible two" years, an oak tree of character is growing. They protect that seedling with patience and persistence, setting limits and coaching obedience.

Teamwork. Now is the time to link arms with your teammate— your spouse. Work together on the race strategy; don't undermine her words and actions. Confer on the rules—outside of junior's hearing. Make sure the boundaries have been clearly marked, then act as if every decision depends on one another's approval.

Faith. When your child is young, begin to teach the faith. Let your toddler see you at prayer. Take your family to church, even if you wind up running relays to the nursery. Teach that little soul to lift itself up to the Creator. Those little eyes and ears absorb a lot. Let them soak in the words and deeds of a faithful dad.

Turns Three and Four: Growing Years

Growing years are equally challenging. Mister Rogers has moved from the neighborhood, and parents are left to answer the big questions. Little hearts are growing and they need tending.

Soon, little Seth and Sarah will learn to ride a two-wheeler. They'll learn how to tie their shoes and button their clothes. They'll also learn how to play with friends without fighting and share their toys without being selfish. And parents will be teaching those classes without adequate salary!

Even so, it's a great time for dads. At turns three and four, a father's role increases in the lives of his children. They need dad more. Here are some of the things you will provide for your family in the growing years.

Boundaries. As children grow, their boundaries expand, but they still need to be defined. Dad will have to raise a few more caution flags—and an occasional red flag. Patience will be as essential as deodorant when wondering minds start testing the fences of do's and don'ts. That's when dad must lovingly remind his children that earth's fences are shields. Boundaries are meant to protect.

Affection. During the growing years, dads will do a few extra push-ups to keep their arms in shape. A little boy or girl needs lots of hugs as they begin to wonder if the world has left them behind. They may hear the haunting cries of a competitor now sleeping in their crib and wonder why their spotlight has been turned off. They'll need to be held closely from time to time—to be reassured that they are still vital members of the household.

Moral Instruction. Along with learning their A-B-Cs and 1-2-3s, kids need to learn the basic building blocks of faith: honesty, love, forgiveness, worship, consideration, and equality. There are lots of lessons to be learned. Fortunately, most of the "students" are still listening through turns three and four. You'll need to be both a moral teacher and a life coach, leading your children through the drills that will form sound character in their young lives.

◼◼◼◼◼◼◼◼◼◼◼◼◼◼◼◼◼◼◼◼◼

Life with Jesus is an endless hope, but life without Jesus is a hopeless end.
—Norman G. Wilson

Lap Two: The Befuddled Years

Parents of pre-teens are usually between thirty and forty-five years old. But nothing in their experience could have prepared them for being the parents of "tweens." They have grade-school and middle school residents in their home, students who barely know how to use a calculator but who can be as calculating as an accountant—and as adorable as a puppy.

As the parent of a pre-teen, you find that Dr. Jekyll and Ms. Hyde have taken up residence in suburbia—under your roof. Suddenly, you find yourself praying for wisdom to St. James of Dobson. Grab the parenting books. Pop in the audio cassettes.

Rewind the child development videos. It's crunch time!

During the "tween" years, unsuspecting dads and moms may not realize that their coaching contract hasn't been renewed. Your child's classmates are now calling the plays. School-time opinions are more important than dinnertime discussions. You may pick the clothes in your child's bedroom, but the real fashion trends are set on the bus and in the homeroom.

And look out. "Birds and bees" are circling for a landing. The cute responses that once satisfied your pre-teen's questions about the human body now require real-life answers. Sleeping glands have been awakened, and their puzzled owners are looking for clues in the fog of preadolescent physiology.

That's when winning dads make their move. Here are the things they provide.

Assurance

Place open arms of affirmation around your pre-teen children. Let them know that they are as important to you now as when you first held them. The malady of "tween" insecurity can be treated with a double dose of loyalty and trust.

Acceptance

It may be hard, but try not to act surprised by anything your pre-teen says or does. "Tween" behavior and dress have the potential to stop a beating heart. The little girl who—just a few days ago, it seems—left the house in frilly lace is now sporting torn denim. The little boy, whose unruly "rooster comb" was carefully coifed with a brush just yesterday, may prefer to have it spiked—or shaved—today.

Behind this bold behavior there is a silent question: "Do you still love me?" For a winning dad, the answer is always "Yes!"

Certainty

Winning dads provide rock-solid answers to the questions of life. They install hooks of certainty where their "tweens" can hang a hat of faith.

Your young adolescent will hear a thousand opinions about God and His Son. Some will be right, others frightfully wrong. Your kids will need a dad who can say with certainty—

- I believe God is, always was, and always will be.
- I believe He created everything that lives and moves.
- I believe that His opinion of us is unchanging.
- I believe that by the sacrifice of His Son, He forgives and forgets our past.
- I believe that He has a purpose for our lives.
- I believe that we are happiest when we follow that purpose.

Boundaries

Dads who survive the "tween" years are those who draw chalk lines on the playing field of life. They determine what's out-of-bounds. Then they watch for infractions and authorize fair but firm penalties. Why? Because their Ariannas and Adams need the security of curfews and other limits. Your children will sense the depth of your love by the length of the rope you allow them. And at some point, you'll probably feel you've reached the end of it!

Lap Three: The Embattled Years

Many parents are living the Middle Ages—theirs! Maybe that describes you. You've accumulated the semblance of a savings account. One car is nearly paid off. You've got friends, some of whom are in high places. You've survived junior high cheerleading tryouts and have won the award for soccer game attendance.

And then it happens.

Suddenly, you find yourself in the straightaway, barreling through life at 200 miles per hour. In the rearview mirror there's another driver who seems intent on passing you at best, sending you into the wall at worst.

Congratulations, Dad. You're the parent of a teenager.

Issues that once seemed simple are now more complex than a phone bill. Up to now, life has been a piece of cake. Now it's more like a jalapeño milkshake! Welcome to the present *tense*.

Relax. You can do it. Here are some things you'll need.

Patience

Do you remember your own teenage years? Recall the time when a pimple on your nose mattered more than a crash in the stock market. Now translate that angst into twenty-first-century terms. That memory exercise builds an invisible bridge of communication—which, by the way, could collapse without warning!

Fairness

When you hand out a punishment, make sure the sentence fits the crime. A fair judgement will be remembered long after the thrill of getting a driver's license is forgotten. If you were a circuit court judge, you wouldn't sentence a jaywalker to life without parole. Then why give a life sentence over a broken curfew or a broken promise?

Composure

The details of an explosive confrontation may drizzle out of a teenager's memory, but the aftereffects of that argument may linger for a lifetime. A war is not worth winning if it means destroying the spirit of your young adult. You've heard the advice, "Choose your battles wisely." That's hard to remember when your teenager emerges from the bedroom looking like a poster child for MTV.

Steady. Breathe deeply. Listen for your heavenly Father's still, small voice. Wait a few moments. Speak softly, slowly. And remember that your teen will probably disagree with whatever you say anyway!

Respect

Mister or Miss Teen probably has had a Social Security card for awhile. They won't draw on it for a long time, meanwhile, they want to begin feeling as if they have some seniority. Winning dads create opportunities for decision making. They learn to give reasonable responsibility with a minimum of kibtizing. Treat your teenager like an adult. He or she may surprise you and act like one!

Lap Four: The Unshackled Years

Making the drive to the college town was as difficult as making the final turn at Darlington with a flat tire. Staggering up three flights of stairs to the dorm room, Dad tries to hide his emotions behind the huge box on his shoulders—the one with the discount store television and the cosmetic case inside. He hopes fellow parents and dorm residents won't be able to distinguish between tears and sweat in the August heat.

The drive home is strange. Quiet. Mom looks out the window to keep her composure. Dad pays more attention to billboards than ever before, trying to keep his mind from wandering back to campus. The child, who only weeks before had waved good-bye from the window of the school bus, has just waved from a college dorm.

The stunned parents turn into the driveway of their *new* home. It's the same address, the same floor plan, and the same square footage. But it seems bigger now. Two minus one does not equal three.

Welcome to the empty nest.

The child that used to be everywhere at once is now nowhere in sight. Parents have just signed off on the product that consumed their full attention for eighteen years. They're in the forty-six to sixty-five mode now. Unshackled.

Deserted is more like it.

Not that there aren't benefits. You enjoy a few dinners out—alone in the restaurant, without fidgeting four-year-olds or fifteen-year-old food fights. You take a vacation—alone in a car without hearing "Are we there yet?"

And then it happens. You're needed again. There's a car loan to co-sign. A wedding to finance. An apartment that needs a new couch—which you carry up three flights of stairs. You've started second-tier parenting. You're present, but at the same time you're absent.

Then you get the positive pregnancy test telephone call—again. This time it's from your daughter, not your wife.

You're a grandparent.

So you start over. Giving instructions. Writing checks. Tending toddlers, "tweens," and teens. Writing more checks.

Your role in lap four is just as exciting—and often as demanding—as the others. Your kids and grandkids still need you. Here's a sample of what you can provide.

Presence

When you're a grandfather, being square is OK as long as you're there. You may not speak the same lingo as your second-tier family, but an encouraging word is timeless in any language. You're in a support role. You'll pace the sidelines like the coach of a basketball team in the NCAA finals. It's your turn to be known as a man with—

- A listening ear.
- A compassionate look.
- A warm hug.
- A congratulatory handshake.

Wisdom

Second-tier families still need first-class faith. You'll need to answer spiritual questions with biblical facts and not guesses. Pray daily for your sons' and grandsons' decisions. Your counsel will guide children and grandchildren to be their best.

Tact

Unsolicited advice from a granddad is usually as welcome as an elephant at an aerobics class. Your children will still want your opinion—some of the time. Watch for the right moment to share the principles that have taken your whole life to learn.

The White Flag: Almost Finished

There may be only four laps for a dad, but they're the most important tasks you'll complete on this earth. And they pass quickly. Sooner than you wish, you'll see the white flag signaling that your work as a dad is nearly done.

Make the most of your opportunity. These are earthly laps that have eternal impact. There are twists and turns, wrecks and restarts, victory lanes and lonely garages. This race is not for the weak at heart. Finishing first as a dad will require you to surrender your human weakness to God's heavenly power.

NASCAR driver Chocolate Myers said, "I believe that God knows what we need, and that if we submit ourselves to Him, then He will supply our needs."[2]

And He will. For prospective dads, new dads, over-the-hill dads, and granddads, God is faithful.

Joe Gibbs Racing Exec Shows Pride in His Children

Steve deSouza and his wife, Missy, are the parents of an older son, Clem, and a thirteen-year-old daughter, Maggie. Steve makes sure his children know that he's proud of them. That pride is communicated through some important dad techniques. "You have to spend time with your children," Steve says. Even in the hectic schedule of motor racing, he sets aside time for his family. Additionally, deSouza says that listening to your children's concerns, interests, and suggestions helps to seal the parent-child relationship. "And don't forget to say 'I love you,'" he adds. Steve also knows the importance of sharing the faith he personally discovered through his friends in the NASCAR community.

Winning Dad Tip

Let your children know you're on their team.

*Winning dads have
the courage to rise
above failure.*

Yellow Flag

*Avoiding Crashes
and Overcoming Failures*

*I've been in two bad wrecks. The first one left me with only a 5
to 10 percent chance of living. I know I'm here today because of
people's prayers. But because of that one decision that day at the
track when I gave everything to Christ, I know that when I do
pass away, I'll go to be with the Lord in heaven.*

—Ernie Irvan, Fifteen Winston Cup Victories

Spinouts add to the excitement of racing. But they're not much
fun for drivers. Often, they result in costly damage to the car—
not to mention painful injury to the driver. Any racing team will
tell you that spinouts and crashes should be avoided at all costs.

That goes for dads too.

Sometimes dads spin out personally—and even crash. Moral failure. Spiritual failure. Financial failure. Family failure. A father's missteps can result in costly emotional damage to the family and even injury to himself.

In a moment of weakness, flesh may rule over spirit, reaction over reason. The incident leaves debris on the track of family life and in the heart. The yellow flag is waved—Caution. Everything slows down while the crash and its aftereffects are cleared. Your personal failure will be devastating to your family. Avoid it, Dad.

But how? In a society where men are surrounded by temptation, how do you remain faithful? In a workplace that's loaded with more tension than a coil spring, how do you keep from popping off?

You start by understanding the reasons men fail.

Understand Why Fathers Fail

David Pearson and Richard Petty were racing side by side up to the last half-lap of the 1976 Daytona 500. In turn four, they made contact. "Petty crashed into the outside wall, then spun into the tri-oval green, scant yards from the finish line. Pearson spun to the pit entrance, made contact with Joe Frasson's car, then spun back toward the race track. Through it all, he engaged the clutch and kept his car's engine running. When he straightened his car out, he was able to stagger across the line and win the event."[1]

It is possible to survive a crash—and even end up a winner. Experienced drivers evaluate every crash for "survivor" clues. Race cars crash for several reasons. As it happens, these are some of the same reasons that fathers hit the wall. Here are some things to beware of in your personal life.

Failure by a Leader

A driver gets loose in the straightaway and taps the wall. The resulting spinout puts him directly in the path of the driver behind him, resulting in a crash. Oil and debris litter the track. Now there's a hazard for every driver in the field.

In the same way, some dads have spun out or crashed because they were following someone who wrecked. Maybe it was a father. He seemed to have it all together: power, privilege, or possessions without limits. He could party until dawn and go to work the next day. Everybody liked him, no matter what he did. But his life followed an addictive pattern. When his son followed in his footsteps, he crashed too.

Maybe it was a friend, like that fellow student who seemed to have a dream life. He was first in his class. Promoted frequently. Elected to office. Popular. Handsome. Charismatic. Articulate. Everyone noticed when he walked into the room. They didn't know about his affair with another man's wife, but you did. He seemed to get by with cheating. You believed you could too.

Drafting is a well-known technique on the racetrack. One driver follows another closely, mere inches from his rear bumper, in order to be pulled along by the rushing air. Beware of drafting in your personal life. Choose carefully when you give your respect. Remember that no leader is beyond failure.

Loss of Focus

Focus is a key to winning races. Darrell Waltrip discovered that during the 1991 Spark Plug 400 at Pocono. Dale Earnhardt Sr. pointed to tire trouble as the reason for falling behind during the race's last laps. But Waltrip remained focused. He said Earnhardt "went into turn one and actually went up on the curve. . . . It made his car jump off the track a little bit and it gave me a chance to get beside him. He was a gentleman about that whole thing. I passed him and checked on out."[2]

Some drivers have spun out or crashed because they didn't stay alert. They took their eyes off the track for a millisecond.

- Exhaust or smoke clouded their vision.
- They looked at the gauges a moment too long.
- They were looking in the mirror instead of the windshield.

Many dads have had personal spinouts because they didn't stay alert to the world's dangers. The "exhaust" of sexual temptation clouded their eyes. The "smoke" of flattery and deceit filtered into their minds like a personal cloud. Perhaps it was a banner ad or an E-mail message that promised pleasure without commitment—free, incognito, password protected, erotic, wild. They bought the moment with a credit card and wound up making payments on a nightmare.

Or they paid too much attention to the gauges—the half-empty checkbook, the over-heated conference room, the not-enough-RPM work production. Worry. Fear. Introspection. Comparisons. They looked at possibilities instead of probabilities. They focused on "what if" instead of "what is."

Maintain focus in your personal life. Here are the gauges you should be reading: your Lord, your wife, and your kids. Don't allow the things that don't matter to take your attention away from the things that do.

Physical Illness

Bill Elliott stayed barely ahead of Cale Yarborough to win the 1985 Southern 500 at Darlington. You might say that a broken hose cost Yarborough the race. After his Ford began smoking in the 323rd lap, Cale said. "There was so much smoke I thought we had lost an engine. But it was only the power steering. After that I had the power to run with Bill, but it was like driving a freight train the rest of the race."[3]

Some racers don't finish because of mechanical failure. They're pulled off the track because something didn't operate properly or failed completely. Engine. Brakes. Steering. Onboard computer.

Similarly, some dads have spun out because of physical or emotional problems.

- Illness.
- Depression.
- Injury.
- Disability.

When an onboard system shuts down in the human body, the race becomes challenging. A costly hospital stay may result. There might be prolonged counseling; physical therapy may be needed. The "driver" may suffer a loss of motor skills or may have physical restrictions.

Families and friends rush to help. They stand by until things return to "normal." But life may never be the same, as medical bills seem like weights around the family's neck and financial insecurity adds to the father's long list of problems. Some families don't survive.

Breakdowns can't always be avoided, but a good crew can reduce the probability that one will occur. A garage that's well stocked with spare parts may make the difference between a minor glitch and a complete breakdown.

There are some things a dad can do to reduce the chance of breakdown. Guard your health. Maintain a family savings plan.

Carry a sensible level of insurance coverage. Nobody can guarantee good health, but a healthy financial reserve can make an illness or injury less damaging to your family.

Weariness

Persistence is a characteristic of winning drivers. It was said of Dale Earnhardt Sr., "Never, never count Dale Earnhardt out of any race. Even under the most adverse circumstances." Earnhardt won the 1993 Coca-Cola 600 in Concord, finishing "3.73 seconds in front of rookie Jeff Gordon as the sun was setting over the 1.5–mile track." The Kannapolis, North Carolina, driver "overcame penalties for rough driving, speeding on pit road and for having too many crewmembers over the wall on a pit stop, and roared back to win."[4]

Some spinouts result from a lack of strength, not skill. Fatigue can take the winning edge off a driver's ability. And the schedule is grueling. Race days arrive with relentless persistence. The team may be fighting mechanical problems in the car and personal tensions in the crew. Problems stack up like a soggy column of uneaten pancakes.

Sometimes fatigue becomes too much for a dad. Problems at work affect the home. World headlines mix with local issues to become a blur of bad news. A weary dad is left vulnerable to frustration and anger. He tries to solve problems with harsh words or swinging fists. A pretty face combined with a listening ear becomes a temptation to unfaithfulness. *Screeech . . . Crash!*

Don't allow yourself to get lapped by stress. Find healthy ways to manage the problems and frustrations that all men face at work. Take time off. Get a hobby. Find a friend to talk to. Most important, recognize when you're mind and body are at a breaking point and give yourself a break—before a personal failure breaks you.

Inexperience

NASCAR historians point to May 29, 1994, as "The day when 'the boy' became a man." That's the day when "twenty-two-year-old Jeff Gordon surprised almost everyone, posting his first NASCAR Winston Cup Series victory in only his 42nd career start by a whopping 3.91 seconds over second-place Rusty Wallace" to win the 1994 Winston at Concord.[5]

Some rookies don't fare quite so well. They spin out or crash because of their inexperience. They don't know the track, the rules, or the moves of fellow drivers. They take unnecessary chances or ignore a spotter's advice. They lack emotional control. They grandstand. Being a rookie is not the problem. Every veteran was a rookie at one time. The problem is *driving* like a rookie.

Some dads have acted like rookies, with disastrous results. They spoke first and asked questions later. They were so busy with their own goals that they didn't learn the "driving habits" of their family. They ran too close to the "wall"—ignoring the advice of older men. Many families fail in the first two years because a young dad isn't willing to adapt himself to family life. Some of them limp to the infirmary. Others just walk away.

On the official race results of life, don't wind up as an asterisk. Being a father is as different from being a single guy as a stock car is different from a go-cart! Slow down. Take some advice from those who have turned a few laps. Find out what your new family needs and how to provide it. Be teachable. You've got a lot to learn.

*No one learns to make right decisions
without being free to make wrong ones.*
—Chuck Milhuff

Determine to Rise above Failure

Most drivers survive a crash. Often, you'll see them racing again a few days—or even hours—after a spinout. In cases where the damage is not too severe, the crew may repair the car and return it to the track to finish the race. Many drivers have won a race even after they crashed on an earlier lap!

Dad, you can recover from a personal crash. No matter what you've done—or failed to do—as a dad, you can go on to win. Here are some things you'll need to get back on the track.

Forgiveness

Remember that failure isn't fatal. Maybe you hit the wall. You broke someone's trust like a stick. You put personal or family commitments on the shelf. You ignored the advice of your friends and set up a tent in the camp of the enemy. But God specializes in restarts. You can still get a victory lap out of life.

That doesn't mean that God ignores the rules. The fines will have to be paid. A driver who breaks track rules may be called to the "little red trailer," the mobile NASCAR, for a powwow with the officials. It may be that you need to make a visit to the trailer of heaven to talk things over.

If you're smart, you'll simply 'fess up.

If you've blown it, lay your fears and failures on the table of God's mercy. Agree with Him that you've done something wrong. That's called *confession*. Make your resolve to turn the other way from now on. That's called *repentance*. And that's all you need.

That's because the fine for your failure has already been paid by Jesus Christ's death on the Cross. You can leave God's trailer without so much as a written warning. He will take that past and put it in a place so far away that you'll never see it. The Bible says that God's forgiveness is so great that it can't even be measured. "As far as the east is from the west, so far has he removed our transgressions from us" (Psalm 103:12).

You may be sitting in the wreck of your life right now. Bruised. Afraid. Humiliated. Worried. Remember that mercy is spelled G-o-d. Forgiveness is spelled J-e-s-u-s, and new life is spelled S-a-l-v-a-t-i-o-n.

NASCAR driver Mark Green says, "Racing is full of ups and downs, and a lot of pressure. But Jesus is the one you can go to with all of your needs and hurts. He's always there for you, no matter what. He is the answer."[6]

That answer is yours for the asking.

Hope

After a crash, don't go to the garage and spend the rest of your days sulking. Get back in the race. Start over. Switch uniforms. Take off the garment of failure and put on the uniform of praise. Races aren't won by drivers who linger in the pits. They are won by those who have the courage to get back on the track.

Never underestimate the importance of experience. It'll help you recognize a mistake quickly and get back into the race!

—Jimmy Johnson

Restoration

A personal failure always results in broken relationships. Those need to be mended. First, restore your relationship with God. It wasn't He who broke things off; you did. He has maintained an open channel of communication through His Word, the Bible. Go there quickly. There are hundreds of promises that seal your salvation. Read them as if your very life depended on it. It does! Hebrews 12:14 says, "Make every effort to live in peace with all men and to be holy; without holiness no one will see the Lord."

Get on the intercom of prayer. Cry out, but don't yell. Your link to heaven is clearer than a digital phone. God can hear the smallest whispers of your heart, and He's always listening. Do some serious talk time. In the very talking, there is release and recovery.

NASCAR driver Mike Dillon says, "I had someone ask me how I handled stress and I had to stop for a moment because that's not a normal question that you get as a driver. I replied, *'with prayer!'* Not only in racing but in everything, prayer is the way to handle stress. Prayer is the answer to everything that we come up against."[7]

Next, you'll need to clear the air with the people you've offended—primarily family and friends. They're hurt, but your openness and honesty will help to heal them. Your honest confession and sincere desire for change will be like an antiseptic to clear away bitterness. And if you've been on the receiving end of a personal failure, let the offender walk! Surrender your right to be right. Forgive. Bundle up the bad times and bury them in the soil of the past.

NASCAR driver David Green says, "You have to be open and realize it's not a perfect world. But as a Christian you know that you can put everything in the hands of God and let Him handle it for you, and rely on God's Word to see you through, whatever situation you are in."[8]

Humility

When you're rebuilding after a failure, work on your serve. That's good advice not only for tennis players but also for road warriors who have spun out or crashed. The repairs have been made. Relationships have been restored. Now focus on helping some other traveler.

Someone you know may be doing hard time in a "cage of consequences." Their own failures have left them spiritually impoverished. You have the keys to set them free. God didn't cause your failure, but He'll use your forgiveness as a shining example that will lead others out of despair. The Bible says, "You ought to forgive and comfort him, so that he will not be overwhelmed by excessive sorrow" (2 Corinthians 2:7).

Look around. There's probably another crash victim in your line of sight. Be a friend. Lend a strong hand or a listening ear. In your humility, you can help others.

Change

You've heard the expression "It's all in your mind." It really is. Have you ever watched an NFL kicker after he missed a field goal? What usually happens on his next attempt? It's worth notic-ing. Before that kicker returns to the field, he paces the side-line—thinking. He kicks a ball into a practice net—thinking. He goes onto the field—thinking. He paces off his approach—think-ing. He huddles—thinking. He looks down at the ball underneath the holder's index finger—thinking. He looks up at the goalposts and down again at the ball—thinking.

And he'll earn more than a penny for his thoughts! His thoughts at that moment are worth a fortune, literally. He's think-ing, "I *will* make the kick. The ball *will* sail through the goalposts. This one *is* a winner." He's not concentrating on the missed attempt. He's thinking about victory.

Here's good advice for dads who've squib kicked an attempt or two: change your mind. Don't concentrate on the past. You can't turn back the clock anymore than you can "take one pill three times a day!" But you can begin again. You can set a new direction to replace your failed course.

You've been on God's pit road where He did more than change a tire. He gave you a new engine in record time! Now resolve to use your fresh start to run in the right direction.

Chocolate Myers reflected, "I used to party all the time. . . . Drinking was my way out, my place to hide. I had the fast sports car and the bachelor pad, but I still needed something or some-one inside to be my best friend, my savior. Christ changed my life . . . It's hard to explain what God can do because everybody has different needs in life. But we all have one need in common: A savior, Jesus Christ."[9]

Go on from here. Clear your mind from thoughts of failure. Make new habits and new friends to go with them. Build into your new life the behaviors that honor God and your family.

Forget the catcalls from the stand and concentrate on the encouragement of heaven. And don't stop until you get to victory lane.

Someone's Cheering for You

A noted country music star became ill just before the grandstand show at a state fair. One of his backup singers, a talent in his own right, was asked to fill in on the spot. The crowd was already in the stands, so something had to be done, and fast! With great reluctance, the backup singer agreed to perform in place of the star.

The stage lights were turned on. The band began their raucous introduction. Then an announcement boomed over the megawatt sound system: "Ladies and gentlemen, we have had a slight change of plan." The substitution was announced. Only moments before, the crowd had buzzed with anticipation. Now, silence moved like a slow-motion wave from the front row all the way to the "nosebleed section."

The band answered their cue for the first song, and the singer gave the finest performance of his career. But the applause was merely polite, at best. Many disappointed fans had already left the venue, disgusted that a substitute was presented in place of the star. The music set was cut short, but not the energy of the backup singer. His attitude was as inspirational as his performance as he sang his heart out, song after song.

Then came the finale.

After the closing song, the wooden stands echoed with the announcer's invitation. "Let's hear it for, . . ." and he gave the name of the brave backup singer who dared to take the stage on that hot August night.

As if they had conferred in a business meeting, the crowd

seemed to be of a single mind. There would be a collective commentary, a silent protest against the promoter who dared to make such a substitution.

The breathless singer took his bow only to be met by silence—terrible, deafening, embarrassing silence. The young man was hurt, but it wasn't anger he felt. It was pain. He had done his best. He hadn't volunteered; he'd been drafted. He wanted to give the crowd a show in place of a cancellation. It was the most awkward and painful moment of his life. Brokenhearted, he turned to leave the stage, a defeated man.

A single handclap broke the awful stillness. One fan rose to applaud. The applause was faint but spirited. It came from the upper reaches of the grandstand, the farthest row from the stage. Then the clapping stopped and a voice boomed over the half-empty grandstand. "Good going son. I believe in you!"

The singer stopped suddenly and shielded his eyes to look past the stage lights and into the stands.

"I'm proud of you, boy!" The father continued, now yelling and clapping at the same time. "I'm proud of you, boy!"

Faces turned toward the sound. Soon, the single handclap became an ovation as one by one, row by row, section by section, audience members stood to affirm the young man's effort. The grandstand reverberated with applause, whistles, and shouts of praise.

A father believed in his son. And that made the difference.

Dad, that's you on the stage. You may be brokenhearted, angry, and hurt. You feel misunderstood, and deserted. You did what you could to salvage a broken situation, but no one seems to care.

Listen!

From the farthest row of heaven, a voice booms loud enough to reach your heart: "I'm proud of you, boy! I believe in you!"

That's what it means to be totally forgiven. You have asked for God's mercy, and it has been given. Your heavenly Father approves of you, even if others don't. He wants you to go on. He wants you to recover from failure. He wants you to finish the race, and He wants you to win.

Ron Pegram Says Stay in Touch

Ron Pegram is director of operations for Motor Racing Outreach as well as one of its chaplains. He says the ministry's philosophy of "hanging out, being approachable, and always being available" to the NASCAR community also applies to parenting. "When you can't be there," Pegram advises, "you can still keep in contact with a cell phone or E-mail." Dad to three grown children, Ron calls at least one of his children every single day.

Winning Dad Tip

Always be available for your kids, even after they've left home.

8

Racer's Edge

*Winning dads
rely on each
other.*

A Winning Team

Mentoring, Partnering, and Male Friendship

At our shop, it's been wonderful to see what the Lord has done. On Tuesday a chaplain comes by for Bible studies, and because of that about twenty members of this crew have become Christians. Now, instead of having a crew that works together as employees, we work together as brothers in Christ.

—Lyndon Amick, 1996 Goody's Dash Series Champion

Seldom—if ever—will you hear a NASCAR driver in victory lane say, "I drove the course like a champion. This was my best performance!"

No. If a sports reporter is lucky enough to make it to the driver— past the sponsor reps, security staff, crewmembers, and owner—he or she will hear something far different: "It was a great race. The car ran perfectly. The team did a great job. I want to thank my sponsors, the fans . . ."

Everyone but the guy ripping tickets at the gate will get a mention. Why? Every driver knows that his success depends upon the work of others. No matter how many trophies may perch on the cupboard of his motor coach, a winning driver realizes that racing is a team sport.

Winning dads know about teamwork as well. They know that making it to the finish line will require the cooperative effort of many people: family, friends, and fellow believers. They understand that every significant *effort* has a significant *other* in the background.

Newspaper columnist and firefighter Isaac Randolph gave heartwarming advice on the value of teamwork in a tribute to a fellow firefighter who had drowned during a training exercise. He wrote:

> While even the most optimistic of us would find it all but impossible to find any good in this tragedy, I think it can be a wakeup call for fathers everywhere. There are lessons for all of us in Paul's too-short life. First, despite what some may think we dads are crucial to the development of our children. We may not be the hand that rocks the cradle, but we can be the hand that builds it. Second, our worth to our children cannot and should not be measured only in dollars and cents. They need our presence, not our presents. Third, we are the first role models for our children. We have the ability to represent the best and worst of what it means to be a man in this society.[1]

And that ability to "represent the best and worst of what it means to be a man" can be fine-tuned through constructive relationships with peers.

Thankfully, the concept of male bonding is a fact of life in our society. Professional football players sometimes hold hands in the huddle. Basketball players hug one another. Baseball players who've made it to home plate can't reach the bench without getting a high five from everyone but the batboy! And a season-full of tension between a rebellious race car driver and a frustrated owner can be melted by a giant embrace in victory lane.

It's OK, guys. We're grown up enough to show our emotional side.

And it's not a moment too soon. People living in the age of voicemail and call waiting need to create opportunities for "face time." As a dad, you can't afford to be as lonely as the receptionist on the thirteenth floor of a twelve-story building. You need strong relationships with other men who will bring out the best in you by the best in them.

You can build those important connections in at least three ways.

Build Lasting Friendships

First, it can be accomplished by forming male friendships. Every dad needs a friend. Many dads would say of their wives, "She's my best friend." *Of course* your spouse is your best friend! That's the whole idea behind an intimate lifelong partnership with another human being. And *of course* you are best friends with other family members. Relationships are the glue that holds families together in the category-five-hurricane environment of these times. NASCAR driver Mark Green says that his wife's friendship and faith have influenced his own. He relates, "I didn't go to church much when I was young, but seeing Christ in my wife showed me just what I was missing and that I wanted what she had."[2]

But dads also need the friendship of other men. There are some times when a man needs the support of another guy who understands what it's like to stand for something in a world that falls for anything. Sometimes you need a friend who knows—

- How hard it is to get a close shave under your neck.
- How to hold a conversation with in-laws and watch a race at the same time.
- That the color of a tie should match the colors in the socks—but doesn't really care.
- That regardless of what the guy on TV says, a "simple" do-it-yourself project will always be harder than putting braces on the teeth of a live shark—in a wading pool!
- That there is someone else who has an inner desire to be an obvious influence for God and for good.

Dads need someone who identifies with them and shares their interests, somebody who can talk about power tools with misty eyes and not be embarrassed. Every dad wants a friend he can punch on the arm without getting a restraining order and one who can listen to complaints about work without filing a grievance. Every dad needs at least one friend who will never tell how small that largemouth bass really was—somebody who will keep a confidence, breathe a prayer, and lend a helping hand—a friend who understands his dreams.

Author Steve Farrar tells of Jeb and Ernie, a couple of good ol' boys who went into the wolf hunting business. A pack of wolves was killing livestock so the local ranchers offered a bounty for every wolf killed. Farrar wrote, "They had been out huntin' wolves all day and into the night, and made camp way up in the mountains near a beautiful little stream. About four o'clock in the morning, Jeb woke up to see their camp surrounded by thirty or forty wolves. In the light of the dying campfire, he could see the blood-lust in their eyes, and the white of their exposed, razor-sharp teeth. He could also see that they were about ready to spring.

"'Hey Ernie,' he whispered, 'Wake up! We're rich!'"[3]

Sometimes a man needs a friend who can help him get back in line after he's hit a speed bump—giving just enough advice but not too much. NASCAR driver Randy Tolsma says, "Be around someone you can trust and look at their life, and see someone who is a believer, compared to someone who doesn't have Christ in their life. Then make a choice. I know what choice you will make."[4]

Where do you find friends like that?

- At work.
- In church.
- In a Bible study.
- At the gym.
- In a civic organization.
- In a service organization.
- In a sports league.

Sometimes a family member provides a shove in the right direction: "You raise aardvarks? So does my brother!" Just about anywhere that people of faith are found you can find a friend.

What do you look for in that kind of friend? You'll want to find someone who—

- Has an obvious love for God.
- Has a good track record for friendship.
- Is known by his good character.
- Cares more about others than about self.

- Treats his family with respect.
- Shares your interest.
- Knows how to keep his ears open and his mouth shut.
- Will lift you up and not tear you down.

With some guys, you may know from the very first meeting whether an acquaintance has the potential for being a friend. With others, it may take months or even years to become best friends. What will that kind of friend be looking for in you? He'll want someone who—

- Listens intensely.
- Tells the truth.
- Keeps communication lines open.
- Understands when he's busy.
- Can tell when an encouraging word is needed.
- Will be on call 24/7.

What do those kinds of friends do together?

- They meet for breakfast, or lunch, or coffee.
- They start a Bible study.
- They pray about the concerns of their families.
- They go to "guy things" together.
- They share family outings.
- They help each other with do-it-yourself projects.

Being a friend "through thick and thin" doesn't have anything to do with weight control. It's a personal commitment by one human being to stand alongside another, no matter what. King Solomon, the man who asked God for great wisdom and received it, wrote, "A friend loves at all times, and a brother is born for adversity" (Proverbs 17:17).

Get yourself a friend, Dad.

It is not what he has, nor even what he does, which directly expresses the worth of a man, but what he is.

—Henry Frederic Amiel

Be a Mentor

Mentoring is another kind of relationship that can benefit a father. A mentor is a teacher, someone who is willing to invest time and knowledge in the improvement of another person—by invitation only. In this relationship, the mentor, usually the older of the two men, offers the benefit of his knowledge and experience to the other. Think of a mentor as a surrogate dad or big brother. A mentor is someone who is willing to say, "Here, let me show you how to—

- Grow as a Christian.
- Be a better husband.
- Improve as a dad.
- Understand the Bible.
- Pray.
- Fix cars.
- Catch fish and build character at the same time.

Mentoring isn't always easy, of course, but it's a great privilege. A mentor must be willing to pour his very life into the life of another and to be patient with that person's weaknesses and shortcomings. NASCAR driver Bobby Hillin says, "Whether we like it or not we're role models, and we have to act accordingly. The best thing is for others to see Christ in us in everything we do. At the track or out in public, we as Christians need to show what Christ has done in our lives to others. . . . We're all role models to someone, somewhere."[5]

Life is a flame that is always burning itself out, but it catches fire again every time a child is born.

—George Bernard Shaw

Who, me? Be a mentor? You're kidding, right?

Not at all. Mentoring is something *you* can do. You've been around the track a few times, so why not share driving tips with a rookie? Whether you have a Ph.D. or a G.E.D. (or neither), your experience can benefit someone else.

Who? Look for someone who—

- Is searching for faith and offer to meet for a weekly Bible study.
- Is struggling with parenting and suggest attending a seminar together.
- Needs a hand with home improvements and suggest a co-project.
- Is struggling with addictive behavior and suggest enrollment in a twelve-step program.

In other words, look for someone who needs a hand with growing up—then offer yours!

Time spent in a mentoring relationship is some of the most valuable time you will ever spend. It's amazing how quickly personal growth carries over from one life to another.

Steve Rabey writes, "Jesus and Paul, the two major figures in the church's earliest years, were hands-on practitioners. Jesus chose twelve disciples, and He invested his life in them for three years. Paul was both an evangelist and a pastor. . . . He also devoted immense amounts of time and energy in shepherding some of the young congregations he had founded and in guiding key leaders like Timothy, to whom Paul wrote these words: 'And the things you have heard me say in the presence of many witnesses entrust to reliable men who will also be qualified to teach others' (2 Timothy 2:2)."[6]

Find an Accountability Partner

A third way that male relationships can contribute to a father's success is by accountability partnering. Accountability partnering is a step beyond casual friendship and even mentoring. It is a commitment between two or more people to submit their lives to each other's scrutiny. When you enter this partnership you voluntarily answer to someone else for your attitudes and actions. The purpose of an accountability partnership is simple: to improve yourself and contribute to the growth of another person.

Being in an accountability relationship requires a significant commitment of time and energy. Whether it's done by phone, E-mail, or (preferably) in person, partners meet to discuss the ups and downs of their personal lives. That can get, well, personal.

"How's it going Steve?"

"Fine, Brad."

"I mean, how's it really going?"

Steve looks a little more intense, "Well, you know the struggle I have with anger. There was an incident this week, at work. You know what a hardnose my supervisor is."

"Yeah, I've heard about him a time or two. What happened?"

"I told him about a discrepancy in an inventory file, and he said there wasn't any discrepancy. In fact, he said he created that file himself, and there wasn't any problem, *period!*"

"And you said?"

"I didn't say anything. I just shrugged my shoulders and walked away."

"Good choice."

"I don't know. I walked away, but in my heart I was ready to go to his computer workstation and break all of his Microsoft windows. He really made me mad!"

"Now that's a problem."

Steve slowly shook his head, "Yep. A problem without a lasting solution, I'd say."

"Except for one."

"What's that?"

"Let's pray for him."

"*Pray* for him? I'd rather punch his lights out!"

"What good would that do?"

"You're right," Steve sighs, "I guess that wouldn't help either one of us."

A moment later, both men bow their heads. In a booth at a fast food restaurant, accountability partners tackle a big issue in a quiet but powerful way.

Brad begins. "Father God, You know the problem Steve is having with his supervisor. I ask you to do a couple of things. First, I pray that you will continue to help my friend deal with anger. Thank you for helping him see that being resentful not only affects his relationship with others, but that it also keeps him from having a joyful relationship with you. I also pray that you will help Steve's boss with the issues in his own life that cause him to react in such a negative way to his coworkers. Thank you, Father, for what you are going to do in Steve's life."

Steve follows, "God, I thank you for giving me a friend like

Brad. I thank you for his honesty with me. I thank you for his commitment to help me with the spiritual stuff. Lord, I do pray for my boss. I don't know what's going on in his life. He may be dealing with some heavy things at home or on the job. I ask you for patience and understanding. I know you're helping me with my anger. I confess my problem to you, and thank you in advance for the changes that you will help me make. In the name of Jesus, I pray. Amen."

One man was accountable to another. The friend wasn't judgmental. He simply asked honest questions. Then, together, they arrived at a spiritual solution.

Accountability partnering takes place during regularly scheduled appointments—weekly, monthly, or otherwise—where two or more friends meet to discuss "home improvements." These accountability meetings have a unique dynamic.

- They are nonthreatening.
- They are goal oriented.
- They are voluntary.
- They are solution oriented.
- They are friendship enhancing.
- They are spiritually beneficial.

Accountability partnering is like directing the flow of a river. A river without banks is a flood. It ruins property, erodes soil, breeds disease, and even claims lives. Riverbanks not only direct the water's flow but also increase its power. In the same way, accountability partnering directs the power of a man; it keeps him spiritually on track.

- It calls attention to harmful things that may be overlooked or ignored.
- It works toward spiritual solutions.
- It creates spiritual alertness.

- It causes personal growth.
- It strengthens friendships.
- It creates positive results in family and professional relationships.

Richard Childress Racing engine builder Lanny Barns speaks of the importance of accountability groups: "We have a Bible study here at RCR each week, and you can see the difference in the team, and in the performance in the race cars on the track. It's really something you can see in all the teams that have Bible studies."[7]

You can bring out the best in yourself by creating healthy relationships with others. Whether it's over a cup of house blend coffee at the bagel shop, in a Bible study at a neighbor's home, or with a burger and fries after a sports event, the time you spend with a friend, mentor, or accountability partner will enrich your life. It will help you be a winning father!

MRO Chaplain Says Know Your Child

Career Highlights

- Lowes Motor Speedway Chaplain

Steve Green, chaplain with Motor Racing Outreach, is assigned to Lowes Motor Speedway in Charlotte, North Carolina. But his duties include much more. He specializes in counseling members of the NASCAR community. In times of crisis, he may be asked to go to one of a number of race tracks to offer a prayer or word of encouragement to drivers, crewmembers, and family members. His most important role, however, is as a father of three and a grandfather of four. "Provide open doors for your children to express their abilities," Green advises. He and his wife Amy practice parenting principles that call for putting preconceived notions about their children and grandchildren aside and discovering their "God-bent"—their own God-designed uniqueness.

Winning Dad Tip

Allow your children to express their uniqueness.

Winning dads love
unconditionally.

The Finish Line

Realizing Your Potential as a Father

There's a lot of different ways to live your life but
there's only one right way, and that's to live for
the Lord.

—Dale Jarrett, 1999 Winston Cup Champion

braham was the ultimate survivor. It is written of that venerable
Bible character, "Against all hope, Abraham in hope believed
and so became the father of many nations, just as it had been said
to him . . ." (Romans 4:18).

God had promised Abraham a son. Yet at more than eighty
years of age, Abraham was seedless in the face of a prophecy that
he would be the father of a great nation. He was a last-place finisher
in the dad Olympics. Yet even though he was closer to Medicare

than to a gold medal, he held out hope that God would make good on His word. And He did; the prophecy was fulfilled.

Abraham had personal faith in an eternal God who does not lie and cannot fail. When he was more than one hundred years old, Abraham became a dad.

Imagine Abraham's journey. It was as if he'd started life on the pole position at Daytona, then spun out on the infield and run last all day. Yet he wound up lapping the field to finish first!

Last to first. That's more than a possibility for twenty-first-century dads. Through personal faith in the Lord Jesus Christ, it's reality!

Bryan Dunaway, rear tire carrier for the #17 Winston Cup team said, "Knowing *about* Jesus was not enough. To know Him is where I found the peace of mind and happiness that I had always looked for."[1]

No matter where you are on the track of life, you can lap your way to a first-place finish. Right now, you may feel like you're so far behind the pack you'd need binoculars just to see the tail pipe of the car in front of you. But you can reach your full potential as a father. It really is possible to be a great dad!

There's a great race-day strategy for fathers in the Owner's Manual for dads, the Bible. It's found in the story of a last-to-first finish of a loving father and his wayward son. That great story has an awesome implication for your life. Let's read it in context, then let's go back for a lap-by-lap commentary. Here's how Jesus tells the story of a father who wouldn't quit—

> There was a man who had two sons. The younger one said to his father, "Father, give me my share of the estate." So he divided his property between them.
>
> Not long after that, the younger son got together all he

had, set off for a distant country and there squandered his wealth in wild living. After he had spent everything, there was a severe famine in that whole country, and he began to be in need. So he went and hired himself out to a citizen of that country, who sent him to his fields to feed pigs. He longed to fill his stomach with the pods that the pigs were eating, but no one gave him anything.

When he came to his senses, he said, "How many of my father's hired men have food to spare, and here I am starving to death! I will set out and go back to my father and say to him: Father, I have sinned against heaven and against you. I am no longer worthy to be called your son; make me like one of your hired men." So he got up and went to his father.

But while he was still a long way off, his father saw him and was filled with compassion for him; he ran to his son, threw his arms around him and kissed him.

The son said to him, "Father, I have sinned against heaven and against you. I am no longer worthy to be called your son."

But the father said to his servants, "Quick! Bring the best robe and put it on him. Put a ring on his finger and sandals on his feet. Bring the fattened calf and kill it. Let's have a feast and celebrate. For this son of mine was dead and is alive again; he was lost and is found." So they began to celebrate (Luke 15:11–24).

A Story with Morals

Have we mentioned that this is a *great* story? It has more drama than any network TV show or *New York Times* best-seller. It is as practical as a toothpick yet as classy as a NASCAR show car. Don't read it and weep. Read it and reap! If you want to finish first with your kids, open the doors of your heart for a life-changing lesson. It has four brief points, but they're more powerful than a stock engine on jet fuel.

Important versus Immediate

First, winning dads always know what really matters. They refuse to let the immediate take precedence over the important.

Jesus continued: "There was a man who had two sons."

The Worth of a Child. Even one son exceeds the worth of the entire U.S. gold reserve! This man had *two!* The Bible says, "Sons are a heritage from the Lord, children a reward from him" (Psalm 127:3).

Anyone who views fatherhood as either a tiresome task or a tax exemption is a thousand miles from the truth. Children are God's championship points. They should be treasured as if nothing else in the entire world is as valuable.

The man in Jesus' story probably would have been listed among the Fortune 500 of his day. He was successful. He had a large estate. He had oodles of property and a gaggle of servants. But he had something even more important—he had children.

What gift has Providence bestowed on man that is so dear to him as his children?

—Cicero

The Issue of Trust. But one day, the hundred to-do items on the man's list (maybe a palm pilot with a foot pedal?) came to a grinding halt on the front porch of the farmhouse. The youngest son, who had spent his few short years on earth helping his father tend the farm, was now "feeling his oats."

The younger one said to his father, "Father, give me my share of the estate."

In other words, "Write me a check, Dude, I'm outta here."

He wanted more than an advance on his allowance. In his heart, that boy had already packed for a trip that would take him far away from his dad's advice. Any father who has held a "front porch discussion" with a rebellious child knows that the journey can begin at about any age!

An immediate reaction might have gone something like this: "Excuse me?! Give you what? H-e-l-l-o! You'll just have to wait for the reading of the will. You'll get nothing but blisters on your backside if you don't get back to work!" The situation could have escalated into a Mike Tyson–Evander Holyfield–style fight (without the ear chewing, hopefully).

But the father focused on the *important* rather than the *immediate*. His child faced an inner struggle. Flying words—or even fists—wouldn't solve this problem. This situation called for a Kodak Moment of trust—trust in the truth he had been taught and in the character that was evolving out of those truths.

So he divided his property between them.

Faith versus Fortune

The *spiritual outcome* of a family is always more important than the *financial income.* Winning dads value family more than money.

Not long after that, the younger son got together all he had, set off for a distant country and there squandered his wealth in wild living.

That's not what the father had planned for his son. He had goals and dreams for the boy. Those goals included more than college degrees and corporate ladder climbing. He wanted his son to inherit faith as much as fortune. He wanted the child to have the comfort of a good reputation even more than the comfort of a new home.

It's possible to have a full bank account and an empty heart. It isn't looks or luxuries that get you through tough times. It's faith. Winning dads want to pass that to their children along with a few dollars. That was not to be. Then, when the prodigal son reached the end of his road, things got worse instead of better.

After he had spent everything, there was a severe famine in that whole country, and he began to be in need.

It's a lesson that every generation must learn. Possessions are fragile; wealth is fleeting.

So he went and hired himself out to a citizen of that country, who sent him to his fields to feed pigs. He longed to fill his stomach with the pods that the pigs were eating, but no one gave him anything.

When he came to his senses, he said, "How many of my father's hired men have food to spare, and here I am starving to death!"

The poor kid. He found out that ordering from the world's menu leaves a bad taste in your mouth. He swallowed the false advertising that promised the time of his life—and he wound up *without* a life. The feel-good promises of earth have no lasting merit. The "real deal" comes from the wisdom and resources of a heavenly Father.

Winning dads know that children need faith more than finances. Winning fathers do everything possible to instill that faith in their kids. How?

- They take an active role in the child's Christian education.
- They set an example of devotion to God and service to others.
- They treat others with the same respect that God does.
- They resolve disputes quickly and in a Christlike way.
- They give more than they get.
- They follow the path that will lead them to heaven, and they take as many as they can along for the ride.

Love versus Judgement

You haven't really lived until you have really loved. Winning dads show their love to their children.

It took awhile, but the boy with shattered dreams finally woke up. When he'd left his father's house, he'd done more than escape a long list of responsibilities. He'd lost out on the love of his family. Ultimately, that love proved to be more important in the boy's mind.

I will set out and go back to my father and say to him: Father, I have sinned against heaven and against you. I am no longer worthy to be called your son; make me like one of your hired men. So he got up and went to his father.

Whatever it would cost, the kid was ready to go home. He needed his dad, and he knew it.

Now comes the good part.

In one of the most poignant scenes in all of Scripture, the love of a father shines brighter than a hundred headlights. The boy had shaken his finger in the face of the one who loved him most. He had packed up his belongings and fled from the only place he truly belonged. He had turned his back on his dad and walked away. Now he wanted to come back.

What's a father to do?

Love First. A winning dad will do what the father in this great story did. He made the decision to let love rule over ruin. The father didn't stand by the gate of his farm with a "three-car grudge." He stood at the roadside with a longing look of hope and love.

While he was still a long way off, his father saw him.

The father was expecting a reunion! He was looking for the best in his child, not the worst. That's a pretty good outlook for any dad. The Apostle Paul wrote, "Finally, brothers, whatever is true, whatever is noble, whatever is right, whatever is pure, whatever is lovely, whatever is admirable—if anything is excellent or praise-worthy—think about such things" (Philippians 4:8). Love makes a decision to look for the best even in a worst-case scenario.

Heart not Head. That dad led with his heart not his intellect. He was *"filled with compassion for him."*

That front-porch argument wasn't important now. It's not that the father had forgotten about it. After all, he was only human. It would have been difficult to forget the harsh words and heartache. But he decided to cover the breakup with a blanket of mercy. Compassion replaced criticism. Love won the battle of the wills. Colossians 3:15 tells us how to make that decision, "Let the peace of Christ rule in your hearts."

The father turned the past over to God. And he left it there. Then he responded to his son with God-given acceptance. Sometimes you have to let God's love forgive others. We don't have that kind of love on our own; it has to come from Him. That's why winning dads lead with their hearts. It's risky, and sometimes painful. It can even be misunderstood. But love always wins.

Shameless Affirmation. What happened next would make a great ending for a Hallmark Hall of Fame movie. The father communicated his affirmation through a display of his affection.

He ran to his son, threw his arms around him and kissed him.

The prodigal son didn't need a lecture. He needed an embrace and a kiss. He needed a public declaration of love. He needed the kind of affirmation that can wrap itself around a rebel and turn him into a son.

In the book *The Call to Contentment,* Norman Wilson recalls the daily ritual of driving his young son to school. The ride allowed a daily chat with the fourth grader, and there was a bonus for Dad. It always ended with an affirmation of their relationship: an expression of "I love you" and a kiss.

But one day the ritual changed. As they approached the school, the boy suddenly realized that his classmates were watching. Embarrassed, he asked his dad if the customary kiss could be replaced by a handshake. Wilson said, "I longed to wrap my arms around him in a father's loving embrace, but of course, I respected his wishes."

That's not the end of the story, however. A joy-filled father relates the happy ending: "The next day, I held out my hand for a shake when to my surprise, my son leaned over for the customary kiss. 'It's okay, Dad,' he explained, 'I've thought it over.'"[2]

Winning dads think it over. And then they decide to openly declare their love and affection to their kids—no matter who's watching.

Restoration versus Rights

Dads who finish first know that settlements are more important than entitlements. They make peace, even when that requires a sacrifice.

The son said to him, "Father, I have sinned against heaven and against you. I am no longer worthy to be called your son."

Somewhere in the back of his mind, the father was probably tempted to cry out, "You're right about that, Jack!

"I worked overtime to buy you that cycle.

"I spent many a sleepless night worrying about you.

"I've gone without, just so you'd have enough."

The prodigal was right. He didn't deserve to be called a son. He had turned his back on the family. He had walked away. He had requested—and received—all that was rightfully his. Dear old dad didn't deserve this grief!

The Question of Relationship. But it's not a story about deserving. It's about forgiving. It isn't about sentencing; it's about settling. So the father settled the question of relationship once and for all.

The father said to his servants, Quick! Bring the best robe and put it on him. Put a ring on his finger and sandals on his feet.

No, he didn't disown his child, although he had the right to. Instead, he called for the symbols of status in the family—the best robe, the ring, and the sandals. He dressed the boy in the finest clothes to make a clear statement: "This is my son!"

Winning dads help their children understand that nothing can possibly place them outside the circle of acceptance. They love their children no matter how unlovely their attitudes or actions may be.

The Question of Restoration. Next, the father settled the question of restoration. Not only was the boy called a son, he was also restored to all the family privileges that he had once enjoyed.

Bring the fattened calf and kill it. Let's have a feast and celebrate.

You can almost read the mind of the prodigal. As he stood there, pale and thin in a robe that seemed too big: "OK, so I'm wearing the best suit. I've got the ring on my finger. But has Dad really forgiven me?"

The answer was in the celebration. This wasn't a pity party to mourn for mistakes. It was a second birthday party. The midnight of the past was gone. The sunrise of the future had dawned. The prodigal son had come home.

Winning dads are more concerned with the future than with the past. They resign the position of family historian and take up the job of research and development director. And a dad that can connect a child's faith with the future is also in the excavation business—he can move mountains! Jesus said, "I tell you the truth, if anyone says to this mountain, 'Go, throw yourself into the sea,' and does not doubt in his heart but believes that what he says will happen, it will be done for him" (Mark 11:23).

The Question of Respect. Respect was an issue too. And the father settled that question in the same decisive way.

This son of mine was dead and is alive again; he was lost and is found. So they began to celebrate.

All the neighbors knew by now. It had been the talk of the town meeting.

"Did you hear about the runaway? He's back."

"I heard he was eating pig food!"

"Disgusting!"

The father knew that the town gossips would have a field day with his son's sad story. That didn't matter. In his heart, his boy was a hero, a survivor of the war on drugs. So Dad decided to be proactive in showing his support by making some public declarations.

"My son was as good as dead, but now he's alive."

"My son was a missing person, but he's been found."

"No matter what you may think of his pitiful past, he's still my son."

"No matter what you may think of his future prospects, he's still my son."

The father knew that by publicly declaring his faith in his boy's "U-turn" he would make a powerful impact on both the young man and his critics. That's an important lesson for new millennium dads. Respect is a life builder.

- Respect the natural abilities of a child and he will develop them quickly.
- Respect the wise choices of a child and she will make them boldly.
- Respect the kind words of a child and he will use them frequently.
- Respect the good friends of a child and she will choose them carefully.
- Respect the honest questions of a child and he will ask them openly.

Respect is the fuel of a child's loyalty and faith. Dads can set rules. But rules without respect are chains that bind, not cords that tie.

A Story with a Twist

The story of the prodigal son is a one of the greatest stories ever told—perfect for a TV miniseries, perhaps. Yet it's a story with an added dimension. It's not just about one man and his son, but about God and His love for each of us.

By offering His own Son, Jesus Christ, as a substitute for our sin, our heavenly Father forever settled the questions of our relationship with Him. We may have packed up our belongings and taken a trip to sin and rebellion, but He stands by the gate of heaven with a longing look and a broken heart. He rejoices when we discover that life without Him isn't really living. The moment we turn to ask His forgiveness, He embraces us with love, pardon, and acceptance.

God has also settled the question of our restoration. Through faith in Christ, we are restored to the family of God. We are entitled to an eternal life in heaven. Our past is buried in a sea of forgetfulness. Then, as Corrie ten Boom, the saintly survivor of a Nazi concentration camp, once said, God puts up a "No Fishing" sign.

God also treats us with respect. Paul the apostle reflected heaven's opinion on this matter in a letter to some new Christians:

> Remember that at that time you were separate from Christ, excluded from citizenship in Israel and foreigners to the covenants of the promise, without hope and without God in the world. But now in Christ Jesus you who once were far away have been brought near through the blood of Christ. For he himself is our peace, who has made the two one and has destroyed the barrier, the dividing wall of hostility, by abolishing in his flesh the law with its commandments and regulations. His purpose was to create in himself one new man out of the two, thus making peace, and in this one body to reconcile both of them to God through the cross, by which he put to death their hostility" (Ephesians 2:12–16).

The Winner's Circle

Dad, the bottom line is this: you can do it! You can be a good man and a great dad. You may spin out along the way, but God will give you the grace to overcome personal failure. You may have to make a few pit stops, asking the advice of mentors and friends. But you've got faith, and that's what it takes to be a winning dad!

Think of it this way: if a stock car driver can reach Victory Lane in a car with no upholstery, no windows, and no air conditioning, you can make it too!

"It's time to pack away those doubts like a 1970s leisure suit and put on the royal robe of faith. It's been freshly cleaned by the blood of the Lamb, pressed by the power of the Spirit in trying times, and paraded down the runways of time with great and mighty success . . . God's not finished with you yet! Jesus Christ has already won your war. You don't have to look very far for a hope over the hardships of time. It's already yours—nonperishable, always fresh, unfading, and it even has your name on it."[3]

You *can* be the father you've always wanted to be! Listen to Heaven's announcer on the radio of your heart: *Green, Green, Green!*

Stan Toler is senior pastor of Trinity Church of the Nazarene in Oklahoma City, Oklahoma, and has written more than forty-five books. He is constantly in demand as a conference speaker, and he taught seminars for INJOY Group, John C. Maxwell's leadership development institute, for several years. Contact Stan Toler at www.stantoler.com or by writing to:

> Stan Toler
> P. O. Box 892170
> Oklahoma City, Oklahoma 73189-2170

Jerry Brecheisen is an author, conference speaker, and musician who currently serves as director of media for The Wesleyan Church. He has written or compiled more than thirty books including *The Call to Contentment*, co-authored with Norman G. Wilson. Contact Jerry Brecheisen at www.brecksong.com or by writing to:

> Jerry Brecheisen
> P. O. Box 6073
> Fishers, Indiana 46038-3528

Preface
1. Scott MacGregor, "Family Ties Pull Tighter after Crash," *The Indianapolis Star*, 5 August 2002, R6.
2. Ibid.

Chapter One: Drivers Wanted
1. Theresa Howard, "Ads Skewer Hapless Guys," *USA Today*, 22 July 2002, 5B.
2. "Single Parent Ministry," Crown Financial Ministries web site, 2002: www.crown.org.
3. Kate Stone, "Irwin's Legacy Lives on for Kids to Enjoy," *The Indianapolis Star*, 31 July 2002, D9.

Chapter Two: You Have a Sponsor
1. "Darrell Waltrip" in *Drivers, Riders, and Teams*, Motor Racing Outreach web site, 2002: www.gospelcom.net/mro.
2. Ibid.
3. Tony Dungy, "Coach Shares Tips to be Great Dad," *The Indianapolis Star*, 16 June 2002, D3.
4. Bob Benson, "What Are You Going to Do about It," *The Heart of a Father: True Stories of Inspiration and Encouragement*, comp. Wayne Holmes (Minneapolis, Minn.: Bethany House Publishers, 2002), 41.

Chapter Three: Owner, Driver, Crew Chief
1. Leonard Pitts, "The Road to Understanding the Value of a Father's Role," *The Indianapolis Star*, 5 August 2002, A3.
2. Ken Canfield, "Challenging Ideas for Action-Oriented Dads," *Fathers.com Weekly*, 8 March 2002. Father Resource Network web site, 2002: www.father.com.
3. Wade Horn, "Finding Deeper Meaning in Life," *The Washington*

Times, 31 October 2000. Reprinted by National Fatherhood Initiative web site, 2002: www.fatherhood.org.

4. "Paul Ward" in *Drivers, Riders and Teams,* Motor Racing Outreach (MRO) web site, 2002: www.gospelcom.net/mro.

5. MRO, *Drivers,* "Hank Parker Jr."

6. MRO, *Drivers*, "Lake Speed."

7. MRO, *Drivers*, "Tad Geschickter."

8. Stan Toler, *God Has Never Failed Me, But He's Sure Scared Me to Death a Few Times* (Tulsa, Okla.: RiverOak Publishing, 2001), 51.

9. MRO, *Drivers,* "Steve deSouza."

10. Source unknown.

Chapter Four: High Performance Hearts

1. Speed-O-Motive, "Engine Building," Racing Help? web site, 2002: www.racehelp.com.

2. Bruce H. Wilkinson, "A Ladder to the Clouds," *The Heart of a Father: True Stories of Inspiration and Encouragement*, comp. Wayne Holmes (Minneapolis, Minn.: Bethany House Publishers, 2002), 77.

3. "Randy Tolsma" in *Drivers, Riders, and Teams*, Motor Racing Outreach (MRO) web site, 2002: www.gospelcom.net/mro.

4. Stan Toler, "Reflecting the Holiness of God," *Journey Into Holiness: Experiencing God's Power for Holy Living*, ed. Norman G. Wilson (Indianapolis, Ind.: Wesleyan Publishing House, 2000), 98.

5. Dr. Peter Hirsch, *Success by Design: Ten Biblical Secrets to Help You Achieve Your God-Given Potential* (Minneapolis, Minn.: Bethany House Publishers, 2002), 115.

6. MRO, *Drivers,* "Robert Pressley."

Chapter Five: Pole Position

1. "Darrell Waltrip," *Drivers, Riders, and Teams,* Motor Racing Outreach (MRO) web site, 2002: www.gospelcom.net/mro.

2. Norman G. Wilson and Jerry Brecheisen, *The Call to Contentment: Life Lessons from the Beatitudes* (Indianapolis, Ind.: Wesleyan Publishing House, 2002), 49.

3. MRO, *Drivers,* "Robert Pressley."

4. John C. Maxwell, *Success One Day at a Time* (Nashville, Tenn.: J Countryman, 2000), 7.

5. MRO, *Drivers,* "Jason Keller."

6. Ibid.

7. MRO, *Drivers,* "Joe Nemechek."

8. MRO, *Drivers,* "Lake Speed."

9. MRO, *Drivers,* "Hank Parker Jr."

10. MRO, *Drivers,* "Dale Jarrett."

11. MRO, *Drivers,* "Paul Ward."

Chapter Six: Going the Distance

1. Jerry Brecheisen, *God's Healing For Your Trauma: A Personal Journey* (Oklahoma City, Okla.: Vibrant Group, 2001), 84.

2. "Chocolate Myers" in *Drivers, Riders, and Teams*, Motor Racing Outreach web site, 2002: www.gospelcom.net/mro.

Chapter Seven: Yellow Flag

1. "The 1976 Daytona 500" in *Great Races,* NASCAR web site, 2002: www.nascar.com.

2. NASCAR, *Great Races,* "The 1991 Sparkplug 400."

3. NASCAR, *Great Races*, "The 1985 Southern 500."

4. NASCAR, *Great Races*, "The 1993 Coca Cola 600."

7. NASCAR, *Great Races,* "The 1994 Winston."

5. "David Green" in *Drivers, Riders, and Teams*, Motor Racing Outreach (MRO) web site, 2002: www.gospelcom.net/mro.

6. MRO, *Drivers,* "Mike Dillon."

7. MRO, *Drivers,* "David Green."

8. MRO, *Drivers,* "Chocolate Myers."

Chapter Eight: A Winning Team

1. Isaac Randolph, "Lesson for All from Dad Who Didn't Return," *The Indianapolis Star*, 18 June 2002, A15.

2. "Mark Green" in *Drivers, Riders, and Teams*, Motor Racing Outreach (MRO) web site, 2002: www.gospelcom.net/mro.

3. Steve Farrar, *Standing Tall: How a Man Can Protect His Family* (Sisters, Oreg.: Multnomah Books, 1994), 220.

4. MRO, *Drivers,* "Randy Tolsma."

5. MRO, *Drivers,* "Bobby Hillin."

6. Steve Rabey, *In Search of Authentic Faith: How Emerging Generations Are Transforming the Church* (Colorado Springs, Colo.: WaterBrook Press, 2001), 197.

7. MRO, *Drivers,* "Lanny Barns."

Chapter Nine: The Finish Line

1. "Bryan Dunaway" in *Drivers, Riders, and Teams,* Motor Racing Outreach web site, 2002: www.gospelcom.net/mro.

2. Norman G. Wilson and Jerry Brecheisen, *The Call To Contentment: Life Lessons from the Beatitudes* (Indianapolis, Ind.: Wesleyan Publishing House, 2002), 81.

3. Stan Toler, *The Buzzards are Circling, But God's Not Finished with Me Yet* (Tulsa, Okla.: RiverOak Publishing, 2001), 212.